ADVANCED TOPICS
IN SCIENCE AND TECHNOLOGY IN CHINA

ADVANCED TOPICS

Zhejiang University is one of the leading universities in China. In Advanced Topics in Science and Technology in China, Zhejiang University Press and Springer jointly publish monographs by Chinese scholars and professors, as well as invited authors and editors from abroad who are outstanding experts and scholars in their fields. This series will be of interest to researchers, lecturers, and graduate students alike.

ADVANCED TOPICS
IN SCIENCE AND TECHNOLOGY IN CHINA

Zhejiang University is one of the leading universities in China. In Advanced Topics in Science and Technology in China, Zhejiang University Press and Springer jointly publish monographs by Chinese scholars and professors, as well as invited authors and editors from abroad who are outstanding experts and scholars in their fields. This series will be of interest to researchers, lecturers, and graduate students alike.

Advanced Topics in Science and Technology in China aims to present the latest and most cutting-edge theories, techniques, and methodologies in various research areas in China. It covers all disciplines in the fields of natural science and technology, including but not limited to, computer science, materials science, life sciences, engineering, environmental sciences, mathematics, and physics.

Li Qi
Hai Jin

Dynamic Provisioning for Community Services

With 54 figures

ZHEJIANG UNIVERSITY PRESS
浙江大学出版社

Springer

Authors
Prof. Li Qi
R&D Center of Internet of Things
The Third Research Institute of Minister
   of Public of China
Shanghai 201204, China
E-mail: qili@mails.trimps.ac.cn

Prof. Hai Jin
Department of Computer Science
Huazhong University of Sci. & Tech.
Wuhan 100037, China
E-mail: hjin@hust.edu.cn

ISSN 1995-6819   e-ISSN 1995-6827
Advanced Topics in Science and Technology in China

ISBN 978-7-308-10576-7
Zhejiang University Press, Hangzhou

ISBN 978-3-662-50551-9   ISBN 978-3-642-34513-5 (eBook)
DOI 10.1007/978-3-642-34513-5
Springer Heidelberg New York Dordrecht London

Preface

The aim of this book is to outline the dynamic provisioning for community services deployed in a distributed computing infrastructure. How to implement a dynamic provisioning and maintenance mechanism in a running distributed system such as a grid, which is to maximize the utilization of computing resources and demands from users, is one of the most important motivations of this book. Another focus of the book is to find out the solutions for improving the availability of the existing grid infrastructure. This book consists of 8 chapters.

In Chapter 1, we give a brief introduction to the history of software maintenance and provisioning. The difficulties and challenges in dynamic provisioning and maintenance will also be discussed. Furthermore, we explore the features of provisioning and maintenance on different distributed systems in terms of various characteristics. The related international standards and implementations are also introduced and compared in the chapter.

Chapter 2 details the basic concepts and principles in grid middleware. After investigating the working mechanism of different grid middleware, we explain the kernel of ChinaGrid and its related projects, which are the fundamental working testbed of the book.

In Chapter 3, a highly available dynamic deployment infrastructure (HAND) is proposed. Six criteria are concluded from practical experience. According to these criteria, two deployment approaches including service-level and container-level are introduced. The analysis of the correctness and availability of the two approaches is presented. From the evaluation results of micro benchmark, service scale and correctness, it proves that HAND can guarantee high availability in a dynamic grid infrastructure.

Using the HAND infrastructure, the focus of Chapter 4 moves to the architecture layer. It concentrates on how to guarantee the scalability and usability of the physical nodes and dependencies among the grid services that are growing so huge. A new architecture named Cobweb Guardian is proposed to resolve this problem. It consists of three executing units in different granularities. In addition, it provides three group-maintaining algorithms to eliminate or reduce the negative affects from deployment, invocation and environment dependencies. The interdependent system services in the ChinaGrid Support Platform are adopted to evaluate the efficiency. The results prove that the proposed maintenance architecture can bring high throughput and availability in runtime.

Sequentially, Chapter 5 proposes a distributed asynchronous maintaining strategy which is based upon the mentioned infrastructure and architecture. The motivation is to reduce the affects from grid heterogeneity and emergent faults during dynamic maintenance. By introducing a three-tier asynchronous model and analyzing the time sequence during the maintenance, the proposed kernel algorithms guarantee that the business logics of upper applications and maintenance will not disturb each other. In addition, the efficiency and availability are much improved. The asynchronous strategy is implemented in the ChinaGrid Support Platform and a practical image processing application is successfully deployed in a grid which consists of three heterogenous clusters. The evaluation results demonstrate that the proposed strategy can improve the efficiency and is tolerant enough of changes in resources and maintains complexity in homogeneous and heterogeneous environments.

In Chapter 6, from the viewpoint of the application layer, we discuss how to efficiently combine dynamic maintenance with two important technologies (i.e., virtual workspace service and interoperation) to resolve conflicts between increasingly massive VO users and resource problems in the grid. Using ChinaGrid and Grid Programming Environment for CGSP (in cooperation with Intel Corp.), the Globus Toolkit 4.0 developed by U.S. ANL, and Unicore 6.0 developed by the German D-Grid are adopted as references. By using the integer programming technology, the dynamic maintenance, virtual workspace service and interoperation technologies are orchestrated effectively and efficiently. In this way, users can finish the job requests even when the resources are inadequate in a local grid. The image processing GridBeans are used for evaluations. The results prove that the proposed orchestration model can efficiently resolve the problem of lack of resources in the grid and guarantee the efficiency of job execution. From the viewpoint of engineering, Chapter 7 details the implementation of all of our aforementioned works. In Chapter 8, we conclude the book and outlook the future challenges.

This book is for researchers, developers and postgraduate students in the fields of grid computing, service-oriented architecture, dynamical maintenance for large, distributed systems. Readers are expected to have some basic knowledge of grid computing and distributed computing.

It is our pleasure to thank the following people and organizations. We are indebted to many former and present colleagues who collaborated on the ideas described here. We would like to thank the experts committee of ChinaGrid, Prof. Ian Foster from ANL, the former and current staff of the ChinaGrid project and the anonymous reviewers for their helpful encouragement and comments. Without them publication of this book would not have been possible. The authors would like to thank IEEE Computer Science Press for permission to reproduce materials in this book.

Li Qi   *Hai Jin*
Shanghai, China   Wuhan, China
April, 2012

Contents

Acronyms

AIX	Advanced Interactive Executive
BPEL	Business Process Execution Language
CA	Certificate Authorities
CDDLM	Configuration, Description, Deployment and Lifecycle Management
CE	Computing Element
CERNET	China Education and Research Network
CFD	Computational Fluid Dynamics
CGSP	ChinaGrid Support Platform
CGSV	ChinaGrid SuperVision
CIM	Common Information Model
CNGrid	China National Grid
CORBA	Common Object Request Broker Architecture
CROWN	China Research and Development Environment over Wide-Area Network
DCOM	Distributed Component Object Model
DMS	Database Management System
DMTF	Distributed Management Task Force
DSAS	Design Structure Analysis System
EGEE	Enabling Grids for E-Science
GCC	GNU Compiler Collection
GIIS	Grid Information Index Service
GJDL	Grid Job Description Language
GOS	Grid Operating System
GRAM	Globus Resource Allocation Manager
GRIDPPI	Grid Parallel Programming Interface
GRIS	Grid Resource Information Service
GRS	General Running Service
GSI	Grid Secure Infrastructure
GRSL	Globus Resource Specification Language
GT	Globus Toolkit
HAND	Highly Available Dynamic Deployment Infrastructure
HDB	Heterogeneous Database

IA64	Itanium Architecture 64bit
IAAS	Infrastructure as a Service
IDB	Incarnation Database
IUDD	Installable Unit Deployment Descriptor
JDL	Job Description Language
JVM	Java Virtual Machine
LCG	LHC Computing Grid
LRMS	Local Resource Management System
LSF	Load Sharing Facility
MDS	Monitoring and Discovery Service
MOWS	Management of Web Services
MSS	Mass Storage Systems
MUWS	Management Using Web Services
N1 SPS	SUN N1 Service Provisioning System
NJS	Network Job Supervisors
OASIS	Organization for the Advancement of Structured Information Standards
OGF	Open Grid Forum
OSCAR	Open Source Cluster Application Resource
P2P	Peer to Peer
PaaS	Platform as a Service
PBS	Portable Batch System
PDS	Progressive Deployment System
QoS	Quality of Services
RLS	Replica Location Service
SaaS	Service as a Software
SOA	Service-Oriented Architecture
SPML	Service Provisioning Markup Language
SSL	Secure Sockets Layer
TPM	IBM Tivoli Provisioning Manager
UDDI	Universal Description Discovery and Integration
UICR	Uniform Interface to Computing Resources
UUDB	Unicore User Database
VO	Virtual Organization
VWS	Virtual Workspace Service
W3C	World Wide Web Consortium
WMS	Workload Management System
WSDL	Web Service Description Language
WSDM	Web Services Distributed Management
WSRF	Web Service Resource Framework

1

Provisioning and Maintenance

Abstract: With the rapid development of computer network technology, more and more businesses need to provide a high-quality and uninterrupted service. However, during the running of the system, the re-configuration of resources, maintenance and update will be necessary. For the traditional services, the system maintenance process might inevitably lead to a decreased Quality of Service (QoS) or even service interruptions. When this problem is injected into a distributed system environment, the heterogeneity of the system and network latency and other issues will make this more difficult to maintain and provision to achieve efficient coordination. On the other hand, even the correct maintenance of the system may lead to non-availability. Therefore, in evaluating how to achieve normal running in a distributed system as well as in a grid management system for dynamic maintenance, in order to satisfy user demand for services, distributed computing has become an important part of research in the field. To well understand this problem, we will introduce the history, background, characteristics and challenges of maintenance and provisioning technology in this chapter.

1.1   History of Software Maintenance

First, we explore the history of software maintenance to understand the necessity of maintenance and its trend in distributed systems.

1.1.1   Maintenance in Software Engineering

Software maintenance was first addressed in the late 1970s (Grubb and Takang, 2004; Lientz *et al.*, 1978). The early research concentrated more on R&D than maintenance. Sequentially, the related investigations and articles were rather few. However, when more and more complicated applications were developed and integrated, the majority of software engineering efforts were for maintenance after deployment. In addition, the recession in the software industry in early 1990s led to a massive reduction in the development budget (Arnold, 1994). The high cost of maintenance and budget reductions in R&D motivated scientists to reconsider the position of maintenance. Today, software maintenance has become a popular topic in the software engineering community. In terms of cost and time, software maintenance in the software lifecycle plays a decisive role.

Software maintenance can be divided into four categories. The first class is the principle of maintenance which includes the definition of the terminology, classifications, software evolution, maintenance demands and so forth; the second is about the key issues of maintenance that involve technological problems, management problems, estimation of maintenance costs, maintenance metrics and so forth; the third part is the maintenance process which consists of six main processes in the maintainance lifecycle; the final class is related to maintenance technologies in processes such as understanding of the program, reverse engineering and re-engineering.

In days past, more and more organizations began to standardize the maintenance work. For example, according to the definition of ISO/IEC 14764[1], software maintenance includes six processes as follows:

• The implementation process includes software preparation and transition activities.
• The problem and modification analysis process.
• The implementation of the self-modification.
• The process acceptance of the modification.
• The migration process.
• The retirement of a piece of software.

ISO/IEC 14764 standard also indicates the four categories of maintenance as follows:

• *Corrective Maintenance*: After the delivery of software, there would be a series of potential defects combined with the release. However, these defects eventually will bring disaster in a specific situation. Thus, corrective maintenance is mainly concerned with identifying the bugs in the deployed software, correcting the defects and debugging.

• *Adaptive Maintenance*: With the rapid development in information technologies, the hosting environment (e.g. configurations of software and hardware) and hosting DBMS (database types, data format, I/O style and storage media) are always heterogeneous. Thus, adaptive maintenance is in charge of making the software adapt to these variations.

• *Perfective Maintenance*: After delivering the software, the end users are always demanding new functions or higher performance. Further processes to meet the demand changes are included in perfective maintenance.

---

[1] Software Engineering—Software Life Cycle Processes—Maintenance, http://www.iso.org/iso/iso_catalogue/catalogue_tc/catalogue_detail.htm?csnumber=39064

• *Preventive Maintenance*: Typically, preventive maintenance is defined as *the methodology of using yesterday's systems to meet the needs of tomorrow*. In other words, it is the use of software engineering methods to maintain a certain software in advance and avoid predictable mistakes.

Statistically, maintenance contributes to about 60% of the software lifecycle (in Fig. 1.1(a)). If we detail the categories (Fig. 1.1(b)), perfective maintenance takes 60% of all maintenance.

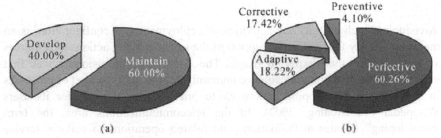

Fig. 1.1. The maintenance ratios

1.1.2 Dynamic Maintenance

Different to software maintenance, dynamic maintenance puts the focus on guaranteeing the stability and correctness of applications during the runtime. For instance, dynamic maintenance monitors the runtime status of deployed software, identifies possible changes to the software, and safely executes the changes at a minimum cost. Broadly speaking, the dynamic maintenance process belongs to preventive maintenance.

The daily maintenance for the computational infrastructure includes service provisioning, configuration management and runtime migration.

• Service provisioning (Stein *et al.*, 2008) is in charge of deploying the new service components, upgrading the existing service components and uninstalling the deployed service components from the computational system dynamically upon the user's demand and QoS requirements.

• Configuration management (Dart, 1991; Estublier, 2000) is responsible for the frequent changes in dynamicity. For example, the newly joined resource node should be added to the serving list for the purpose of prompt invocation.

• Runtime migration (Chen *et al.*, 2006) is for cloning a proper instance of some service components to a new computational node. This functionality is usually required for fault tolerance and a highly reliable system.

Due to the nature of dynamic maintenance, it pursues keeping the synchronous status of software instances among target systems. To guarantee this, we need three prerequisites as follows:

• A software system should show integrity during and after the maintenance process.

• The status of running instances inside the software system should be synchronized after maintenance process.

• After maintenance processing, the software system should be correctly and stably running according to the original purpose of maintenance.

1.2   Maintenance Provisioning

Provisioning, including its sub-activities of deployment and configuration, is an important activity that is done in support of the self-managing actions as resources are prepared for their expected usage. The concept of provisioning was first proposed by the telecommunications community, which refers to a set of processes for preparing and equipping a network to provide new services for its users (Wikipedia Provisioning, 2002). In the telecommunications area, the term "provisioning" equates to "initiation" and related operations to make a service available. According to the discussions in Section 1.1.1, provisioning in a narrow sense will be the first process (i.e., *the implementation process includes software preparation and transition activities*). However, in distributed environments with massive community services, the lifecycle of each service would be unclear due to the continuous integration, upgrade and release of newer version candidates. Generally, the provisioning procedure for distributed community services has the following characteristics:

• It exists in all processes of software maintenance. Any modification, retirement and preparation of services require the provisioning system monitoring the status of target services and determining sequential operations according to the states.

• It manages all related software and hardware resources in a global view to keep synchronization among distributed services.

• The provisioning processes should be as adaptive and preventive as possible. Namely, the provisioning operations can be viewed as a special case of adaptive and/or preventive maintenance.

• Most important, the provisioning processes concentrate more on dynamicity in real time. The characteristics of correctness, availability and safety hold much more important positions than normal maintenance.

With the popularity of cloud computing, the provisioning technology becomes essential to construct an on-demand, adaptive and reliable distributed computing system. In terms of provisioning targets, we can classify the provisioning works as server and user provisioning in the following sections.

1.2.1   Server Provisioning

Dissimilar to a desktop computing system, typical distributed computing demands massive software components collaborating in parallel to resolving complicated problems on time. However, this requirement is more and more challenging with the growth in scale of a computing system. Thus, the preparation of a distributed application infrastructure which normally is composed of a bunch of servers is called server provisioning (Machida *et al.*, 2008; Villela *et al.*, 2007). The specific operations include:

• Choosing a group of available servers from a pool of grid nodes.

• Installing corresponding software which supports the execution of the application. This software includes the operating system, device drivers, middleware, database management system and applications.

• Setting up the configurations of the installed software to guarantee the correct execution. The configurations include networking setup, middleware configurations and critical applications' attribute files.

• Activating and starting up the applications running on the servers.

• Monitoring the servers and executing corresponding maintenance works periodically.

• Finally, when the lifecycle of the application is ended, a series of operations include tearing down applications, uninstalling and releasing the resources back to the available grid pool.

Although provisioning a PC server, the related processes are relatively simple. However, when the provisioning targets are shared with thousands of users, a host of new problems arise.

• The sharing mechanism is important at the infrastructure level. Because the end users in different domains share a common computing infrastructure, thousands of running software programs in different lifecycle stages should be effectively isolated during provisioning processes. This applies to any specific software at any moment.

• The functions of provisioning should be scalable and extendable to different categories. In addition to maintenance works, software provisioning has been designed to resolve new problems such as load balancing, self-evolution and dynamical job scheduling (Urgaonkar *et al.*, 2008).

• With an increase in heterogeneous resources, software provisioning demands timeliness, fault tolerance and transparent processing of underlying heterogeneous resources (Stein *et al.*, 2007).

1.2.2 User Provisioning

Similar to server provisioning, user provisioning is also a preparation procedure to help end users more quickly, economically and securely construct their application environments. It also needs to prepare the operating system, database and configuration files that support running users' applications. However, user provisioning concentrates on user level logic and the quality of services (Mitsos *et al.*, 2004). In particular in this book, we define user provisioning as the preparation of users' applications in a common infrastructure. For example, we plan to provision an image processing service on a cluster with 30 grid nodes. The user provisioning in this scenario refers to the deployment of software, configurations of the services and activation of related image processing services. The provisioning processes for underlying infrastructure, which include networking, operating system and middleware, are not classified in this scope.

One of the advantages of user provisioning is that end users can put their focus on the user-level logic instead of complicated maintenance for infrastructure-level maintenance. Although end users lose the chance to optimize lower level resources for their applications, the transparency can save much time in design and maintenance at the system level. Furthermore, since this kind of provisioning is transparent for the upper logic of applications, the server provisioning services can be more professional for self-management and make the computing infrastructure easier to manage.

Upon the introduction of maintenance and provisioning, it is not hard to find that there is a clear difference between the maintenance and provisioning processes. One of the key differences is that the former process concerns daily operations, whereas the latter is concerned with software engineering. For this reason, we will use the two terms alternatively in this book.

1.3   Characteristics and Challenges

In this section, we explore the characteristics and challenges in dynamic provisioning.

1.3.1   *Provisioning Characteristics*

C'erin and Koskas (2005) indicated that large-scale systems such as the grid have seven main properties: scalability, heterogeneity, availability, fault tolerance, security, dynamicity and usability. Mapping these properties to provisioning, we conclude that the characteristics of distributed and dynamic provisioning are as follows:

• *Scalability*: The maintaining instructions can be correctly propagated to thousands, even millions of nodes. At the same time, provisioning processes should adaptively handle the growing dependencies among the invocations, services and environments.

• *Heterogeneity*: To maintain the services and software correctly, the provisioning processes should consider multiple policies for the different nature of software and hardware. For instance, it should deal with different operating systems (e.g. Windows, Linux, AIX and so forth), different architectures (e.g. x86_32, IA64, x86_64 and so forth), and different compiler versions (e.g. GCC 2.1 and GCC 2.3). In addition to the physical resources, the synchronizing time decided by networks, i.e., package transferring time and instruction executing time also need to be concerned in the provisioning policies.

• *Availability*: The provisioning processes should be completed in the meantime to guarantee the minimum system downtime for end users.

• *Fault Tolerance*: Some uncertain factors including unstable network latency and emergency events make it harder to quickly and correctly propagate the provisioning tasks to each grid node. The provisioning system should tolerate the faults and guarantee the correctness of each execution.

• *Security*: The provisioning should be strictly authorized to the trusted members of Virtual Organization (VO).

• *Dynamicity*: The provisioning system should guarantee the correctness of maintenance when the grid nodes leave or join occasionally during the runtime.

• *Usability*: The provisioning interface should be simple. In addition, the propagation of instructions should be transparent to the end users.

Statistically, characteristics of *heterogeneity* and *fault tolerance* bring more troubles to distributed systems. Because when various grid services have been provisioned to handle large-scale distributed resources, the provisioning processes suffer from high inconsistency and complicated dependencies.

1.3.2 Challenges

Although dynamic provisioning concentrates the runtime and dynamicity, there are several practical challenges as follows.

1.3.2.1 Hot Deploy-Enabled Infrastructure

The hot deploy (replacement) technology is rather critical to dynamic maintenance. Without shutting down a software system or a physical server, how to safely replace the maintaining targets is very important to enhance the efficiency of maintenance.

Some popular software architectures such as DCom, CORBA (Pellegrini, 1999) and JVM (Ao, 2000) support the hot replacement of components.

Specifically, Ao (2000) proposed a hot swap strategy to enhance the software maintenance processes. It provides an auto-managed framework where the subset of software can be reconfigured on a component-by-component basis while the global software execution consistency is guaranteed.

1.3.2.2 Dynamic Reconfiguration

Dynamic reconfiguration (Boari *et al.*, 2008; Smith and Anderson, 2004; Smith *et al.*, 2004) in a distributed system means that the system can continuously evolve without recompiling and restarting after reconstruction. Different to the designing phase, the effects brought about by dynamic reconfiguration of the target system will be minor. Sequentially, the system can keep providing services without rebooting.

Kramer and Magee (1985; 1990) discussed many theoretical practices for the provisioning of a dynamic distributed system. In their works, the distributed system is described as a direct graph and graph nodes are entities connected by links. In this model, they assume that there is at most one connection between the entities. In addition, the entities can only interact through their respective states. Between the two entities, the transaction can only be activated by one of the entities. Furthermore, they defined the dependencies between the transactions. For instance, the transaction t depending on transaction t_1, t_2, t_3, ... , t_n means t can be executed only after all of the preceeding transactions are completed. Accordingly, even a minor dynamic deployment operation will cost much on a running software. On the other hand, the complexity also brings troubles for the application designer who should consider many more runtime situations for possible maintenance.

Moazami-Goudarzi (1999) proposed an optimized approach. By assuming that the system does not support multiple transactions (i.e., a single component can only occupy one transaction), the system can put the component into a passive status when it is not in any transaction. The advantage of this approach is that an administrator need not actively enforce a component into the passive status. However, the scope of available components is limited because any component cannot occupy two or more transactions at the same time.

In Bidan *et al.* (1998) investigation, the dynamic maintenance function is not implemented in the middleware layer. Besides, it needs a remote invocation from client applications or services to activate. However, the server-side or the client-side should be designed in a multi-thread style.

However, all of these solutions can not efficiently provision the components in a service-oriented, dependent and distributed environment.

1.3.2.3   Detection and Optimization for Service Dependency

Generally, large-scale grid services are constructed by massive remote service components that are deployed in geographically distributed computing resources. This loosely coupled architecture reduces computing resources' availability and reliability. In addition, it brings a higher cost of administration and maintenance. For example, a distributed execution system normally equips some data centers and information centers. During the period of maintaining the information centers, the execution system might totally stop due to the sequential dependency. Also, if the maintenance processes experience a failure, the system will reject all of the requested services. Furthermore, if the system implements the stateful services like the resources in Web Service Resource Framework (WSRF), the statuses among distributed service components might be asynchronous, which eventually would make the computing results unpredictable.

Because of these problems, the correct maintenance for the distributed service components is not only a simple hot swap task. Thus, a dependency model is necessary to describe the runtime dependencies among distributed service components to help administrators analyze the statuses of a distributed system.

Chu *et al.* (2005) proposed a dependency isolation mechanism, named as a dependency capsule, to improve the availability of multi-thread based Internet services. They discussed three kinds of service dependency (aggregating, bypassable and replication dependencies). Nevertheless, they did not explore the application of the deployment problem. Their focus is on the runtime to avoid the availability of a multi-thread based system when a block happens.

Sangal *et al.* (2005) invented a dependency structure matrix to describe the dependencies among legacy software. It is efficient to explore the software architecture from the view of software engineering. But they did not discuss the stateful dependency and how to generate efficient deploying solutions. Furthermore, the dependency structure matrix is not convenient for dynamic deployment in grids.

The Progressive Deployment System (PDS) (Alpern *et al.*, 2005) was developed from the viewpoint of a virtual machine. Tolksdorf (2002) defined a dependency markup language for Web services. These solutions do not consider the variable dependency and the optimized deployment solutions for stateful grid services either.

1.3.2.4 Heterogeneity and Fault Tolerance

In the traditional solutions, maintaining the system in a synchronous way is adopted by major maintenance workflow systems or virtual management systems that propagate the daily maintaining instructions for a distributed environment. In this way, for each maintenance, the provisioning system transfers the related configurations or packages to remote resources first, and then executes the maintaining operations. After propagating all the maintenances to the target, it executes the next maintenance in the scripts or workflows. Normally, the maintaining time is decided by the package transfer time and the actual execution time of each maintenance. The two factors are unpredictable due to unstable network bandwidth, the processing capability of target resources and the availability of target resources. In particular, it cannot promise consistency when emergencies happen.

To handle the heterogeneity and fault tolerance problems, dynamic provisioning and maintenance should meet the following requirements:

• The maintenance system should provide a mechanism to guarantee the maintaining processes are safe and reliable. Sequentially, the minimum stopping time and fault tolerance capability can benefit the users and administrators.

• On the other hand, the maintenance system can provide some strategies to keep the normal execution procedure and maintenance procedure synchronized. Eventually, the system can intelligently analyze the maintenance on demand.

1.4   Distributed and Service-Oriented Dynamic Provisioning

In this section, we will introduce the provisioning targets and explore different provisioning features for those architectures.

1.4.1   *Target System*

As depicted in Table 1.1, there are mainly four distributed systems (Foster and Kesselman, 1998; Mugler *et al.*, 2005; Ripeanu *et al.*, 2002) that demand dynamic provisioning technologies. The four systems are cluster, grid, peer-to-peer (P2P) and cloud.

Table 1.1   Maintenance in four distributed architectures

	Cluster	Grid	Peer-to-Peer (P2P)	Cloud
Granularity	Applicability	Node-level	Node-level	Node-level
Hetero. Prov.	Small, lower cost	Big, higher cost	Neutral, neutral cost	Big, lower cost
Intelligent	Lower	Higher	Higher	Higher
Representative	OSCAR, OpenPBS	LSF, Sun Grid Engine, CGSP, GT, SmartFrog	PROST, Gnutella	Rightscale, Elastra, Kaavo, CohensiveFT
Re-configurability	Strong	Strong	Weak	Strong
Topology	STRCT	Tree STRCT	NonS/STRCT	NonS/STRCT
Upper applications	Multiple	Multiple	Unique	Multiple
Applications	Data, computing intensive	Computing intensive	IO flow intensive	Computing intensive
Dependency	Strong	Strong	Weak	Strong
Maintenance cost	Small	Neutral	Big	Neutral
Synchronization	Sync	Sync and Async	Async	Async and Sync

STRCT: Structured; NonS: Non Structured; Async: Asynchronous; Sync: Synchronous

1.4.1.1   Cluster

Cluster computing first appeared in 1960s. IBM was committed to deploy scientific computing to a cost-effective commercial model. When efficient microprocessors, high-speed networks and high-performance toolkits in a distributed environment were available at a reasonable price, cluster computing experienced a rapid development in the 1980s.

With the commercial success of cluster promotion, the resource management of cluster computing became a hot research topic. Naturally, as a core technology, the dynamic maintenance of resource management became an essential investigation point.

Currently, the cluster platform can be deployed with various operating systems, such as Linux (Bollinger, 1999), Solaris and NT (Tingey, 1998). For these systems, a bunch of dynamic maintenance tools and resource scheduling tools were proposed in the form of middlware. The examples include Condor (Adabala *et al.*, 2000), Portable Batch System (PBS), Load Sharing Facility (LSF) (Wei *et al.*, 2005) and so forth.

The commonsense link between dynamic provisioning and resource management is to efficiently and safely allocate computing resources and service components for the deployed applications. The main approaches to maintaining the cluster resources include (i) discovery and communication specification, (ii) dynamically matching of available computing resources and (iii) an on-demand schedule.

1.4.1.2   Grid

In the late 20th century, the grid system (Foster and Kesselman, 1998; Foster *et al.*, 2001) was proposed for complicated scientific computing applications. The definition of a grid is "*a large-scale geographically distributed hardware and software infrastructure composed of heterogeneous networked resources owned and shared by multiple administrative organizations which are coordinated to provide transparent, dependable, pervasive and consistent computing support to a wide range of applications*" (Miguel and Yannis, 2004). As grid computing has great potential for large-scale distributed applications, many countries have invested in building a nationwide grid system. The examples include the NASA's Information Power Grid (IPG) (Johnston *et al.*, 1999), TeraGrid (Reed, 2003) in the U.S., Enabling Grids for E-Science (EGEE) (Blanchet *et al.*, 2006; Coles, 2005; Gagliardi and Begin, 2005) in the E.U., and ChinaGrid (Jin, 2004), CNGrid (Gong *et al.*, 2003; Yang *et al.*, 2005) in China. The research of the grid community has widely covered management layers, communications, resource allocation, job scheduling, security and authorizations. Obviously, dynamic provisioning in runtime is one of the most important fields because the nature of the grid is to efficiently coordinate the available resources in a meta-computing environment. We will introduce the grid technology in detail in Chapter 2.

1.4.1.3   Peer-to-Peer System

Peer-to-peer (P2P) technology was first proposed in the 1960s. It equips a distributed network architecture whose participants make a portion of their resources available to other participants, without central coordination. The earlier forms of the P2P network are Telnet and the electronic mailing system. Because the P2P nodes do not need a central service (such as Grid Resource Allocation Management Service), the capability of the P2P network increases much. However, the loosely coupled networking style leads to challenges in maintenance. Even a simple upgrading process of some critical component will be a disaster for the P2P system, because nothing can guarantee the synchronous status of related service components. With the growth in scale of popular P2P networks (Cochrane, 2001; Ripeanu *et al.*, 2002), dynamic maintenance technologies have been widely discussed (Benatallah *et al.*, 2003; Liben-Nowell *et al.*, 2002).

1.4.1.4 Cloud System

Cloud computing (Armbrust *et al.*, 2009; Buyya *et al.*, 2009), proposed early in the 1960s, proposes to publicly share the hardware, systems software and applications as services over the Internet. The popularity nowadays of cloud computing started from 2000. Amazon and Google (Ghemawat *et al.*, 2003) played an important role in developing cloud system services. By dividing the architecture into several layers, cloud computing proposed the *Infrastructure as a Service* (IaaS), *Platform as a Service* (PaaS) and *Software as a Service* (SaaS). With these services, different users can conveniently construct their cloud applications on demand over the Internet. By facilitating a virtual machine (Goldberg, 1976), MapReduce (Dean and Ghemawat, 2008) and Web services technologies (Dustdar and Schreiner, 2005), cloud computing can provide an extremely agile computing infrastructure according to end users' demands (Konstantinou *et al.*, 2009). The typical systems include Rightscale (Dean and Ghemawat, 2008), Elastra (2009), Kaavo (2009) and Cohensive (2009).

1.4.2 Related Products

Dynamic maintenance technology has been widely implemented by industry and academic institutions for different distributed systems.

1.4.2.1 Provisioning System for Cluster

In the scientific computing area, the successful representative is Beowulf, a high-performance cluster management system. It was initially developed by Goddard Flight Center, NASA. Naturally, the main goal is to support large-scale scientific computing, such as geographical and spacial computing challenges. Inside the Beowulf cluster, one of the most popular maintenance softwares is the Open Source Cluster Application Resource (OSCAR). It is dedicated to making the complicated installations in clusters as easy as in a desktop computer (Denneberg and Fromm, 1998; Mugler *et al.*, 2005). Otherwise, the OSCAR project aims to support different Linux distributions as many as possible.

Supported Linux distributions as mentioned on the OSCAR Website are Debian, Fedora, OpenSUSE, Red Hat Enterprise Linux and Ubuntu.

Another popular maintenance toolkit for clusters is Redhat Package Manager (RPM), a simple software package management software. It provides an easy and efficient management mechanism for a single node system.

1.4.2.2 Maintenance System for a Grid

Table 1.2 concludes some popular maintenance systems in terms of some qualitative capabilities (Blanchet *et al.*, 2006; Caromel *et al.*, 2007; Reed, 2003).

Table 1.2 Comparisons between different grid maintenance tools

Testbed	MW	Main Tool	Qualitative Characteristics						
			SCA	HET	FT	SEC.	DYN.	ACC.	AVAL.
TeraGrid	GT2, GT4	VWS GridFTP+RFT	High	support	neutral	GSI	Neutral	API Portal	High
EGEE	GT2, gLite	SmartFrog	High	Linux	Neutral	GSI	Neutral	API	Neutral
D-Grid	UNICORE	Unix	High	Support	Neutral	SSH	Neutral	GUI	Neutral
Grid5000	ProActive	KA-deploy	High	Linux	Neutral	SSH	Neutral	Portal	Neutral
ChinaGrid	CGSP2	HAND Guardian	High	Linux	Neutral	GSI	High	API GUI Portal	High
CNGrid	GOS2.1	Linux	Support	Neutral	Neutral	GSI	Neutral	Portal	Neutral
IBM	WAS	Tivoli	—	Support —	—	—	—	—	—
SUN	SGE	N1 System	High	Support —	—	—	—	—	—
HP	GT4	SmartFrog	High	Support	Neutral	GSI	Neutral	API	Neutral

MW: Middleware; SCA: Scalability; HET: Heterogeneity; ACC.: Access; FT: Fault Tolerance; SEC.: Security; DYN.: Dynamicity; AVAL.: Availability

Keahey *et al.* (2005) proposed the Virtual Workspace Service (VWS) for Globus. It equips the virtual machine technologies (e.g. Xen and VMware) to provide an agile and on-demand allocation mechanism in grids. Namely, VWS deploys the virtual machine images instead of service components into hosting resources. The advantages of VWS include: (i) It can rapidly construct a relatively complicated workspace for scientific computing applications without considering the different internal logic. (ii) It can adaptively deploy the applications according to their size and users' demands. (iii) The working space can be easily stored or recovered. However, the weakness of VWS is the huge cost of storage and network bandwidth for transferring images on the Internet. Currently, as an optional component of Globus toolkit, VWS has been accepted by TeraGrid.

EGEE is one of the biggest grid projects funded by the European Commission. It hired the LCG-2 based on GT2 and gLite as the middleware to manage the grid resources. For maintenance purpose, the SmartFrog (Sabharwal, 2006) from HP Labs has been adopted. SmartFrog is designed and implemented according to Configuration Description, Deployment, and Lifecycle Management (CDDLM) specification which is an Open Grid Forum (OGF) standard for the management, deployment and configuration of grid service lifecycles or inter-organization resources. This standard provides a framework which describes a language and the methods that have the ability to describe system configuration and move the system, services and software towards desired configuration endpoints.

INRIA Grid 5000 is the grid infrastructure in France. It takes a script-based toolkit, named KA Deployment (Caromel *et al.*, 2007), as its maintenance system. The users can customize the size of computing resources according to their application demands by using KA Deployment. KA's maintenance targets include kernel OS (normally Linux) and binary applications. Similarly, the German D-Grid developed UNICORE middleware on Unix/Linux.

In China, many grid projects also equip the distributed, service-oriented and dynamic maintenance technologies. The maintenance technologies in this book have been accepted by the ChinaGrid Support Platform (CGSP). From the infrastructure to the architecture, CGSP can easily manage massive service components from ChinaGrid's five application grids.

Similarly, the VEGA grid operated by the Institute of Computing Technology, Chinese Academy of Sciences is also a representative of the service-oriented grid (Gong *et al.*, 2003). Although VEGA did not follow the WSRF specification, it developed a standalone maintenance toolkit based on Apache's AXIS engine.

ROST (Hailong *et al.*, 2006), deployed in the CROWN grid, focuses on dynamic and remote deployment for the WSRF core with secure access. The developers evaluated remote deployment in the load balancing of local clusters.

In the industry, many enterprises implemented several production level maintenance tools. There are HP's SmartFrog, IBM's Tivoli Provisioning Manager (TPM), built on SOA principles, which enhances usability for executing changes while keeping server and desktop software compliant (Shwartz *et al.*, 2005). TPM helps organizations with provisioning, configuration and maintenance of servers, virtual servers and other resources. It supports operating system provisioning, software provisioning and storage provisioning.

SUN N1 Service Provisioning System (SPS) automates the deployment of multi-tier applications across heterogeneous resources (Zielinski *et al.*, 2005). The highlight of N1 SPS is that it can simulate the deployment process on target systems prior to actually implementing the changes to ensure successful delivery. In addition, the version control and role-based access control can help users construct applications efficiently.

In addition, Javadpour (2001) invented a software management model to handle the dependencies among components to automatically upgrade the deployed components.

Correct and efficient analysis of software structures is the basis for system maintenance. Rusnak (2005) proposed and evaluated an advanced analysis tool for a software structure, called the Design Structure Analysis System (DSAS). DSAS records all of the dependencies in a design structure matrix. Sequentially, it adopts a special algorithm to analyze the target software component structure.

1.4.3 Related Standards

The investigation of deployment and management for distributed software packages has been rather popular recently. W3C released the Installable Unit Deployment Descriptor (IUDD) specification to describe the distributed software packages. It describes the static dependencies among software packages. It can't adapt the dynamic changes during the runtime. Moreover, IUDD can't generate the deploying workflow for distributed nodes (Draper *et al.*, 2004).

CDDLM specification discussed in Section 1.4.2.2 is dedicated to providing a set of adaptive solutions for distributed software deployment and configuration management on experienced demand. However, it is a specification of the deployment infrastructure. It considers how to combine the deployment infrastructure with the runtime execution system and support the dynamical variety of the configuration. In addition, it investigates less the dependency among the services, especially the stateful dependencies.

The Organization for the Advancement of Structured Information Standards (OASIS) released a standard providing an XML framework for managing the provisioning and allocation of identity information and system resources within and between organizations, named Service Provisioning Markup Language (SPML). The SPML model consists of four main roles: Requesting Authority, Provisioning Service Provider, Provisioning Service Target and Provisioning Service Objects. It defines the communicating protocols between these roles. In addition, OASIS released Web Services Distributed Management(WSDM) specification which consists of Management Using Web Services (MUWS) and Management of Web Services (MOWS). The WSDM specifications are designed to manage the distributed service components in a standard model.

1.5 Summary

To meet the new needs and to adapt to the constant development of new technologies and the emergence of a new environment, most of the software systems in their lifecycle experience several revisions and changes. However, if the administrators turn off and restart them, it may bring unacceptable delay, high cost or non-exposure. Thus, for economic (such as e-commerce, banking, securities, etc.) or security (national defense, etc.) reasons, we can't stop these key business systems (such as traffic control, telephone exchanges or some high-availability public information systems) modifying and changing existing components or subsystems. This must be dynamically done during operations to maintain and update the configuration. Changes to the system not only are made by external entities such as users or system designers, but also may be continuous advancements in technology to promote the inherent dynamic updating of the system itself. Sequentially, studying the mechanism for dynamic maintenance of essential services to improve the availability and reliability remains important.

With more and more scientists sharing advanced computing facilities such as EGEE, TeraGrid, ChinaGrid and CNGrid, the necessity to enhance the maintenance technologies on those distributed infrastructures is rather important. This study points to maintenance and provisioning technology including improving the availability of computing facilities to overcome the heterogeneity of computing platforms, increasing the platform's ease of use, security, scalability, fault tolerance and dynamic nature. We will detail these challenges in this book in terms of infrastructure, architecture, strategy and application level to achieve these characteristics.

References

Adabala S, Kapadia NH, Fortes JAB (2000) Interfacing wide-area network computing and cluster management software: Condor, dqs and pbs via punch. In: Kesselman C, Dongarra J, Walker D (eds.) The 9th International Symposium on High-Performance Distributed Computing, 2000. IEEE Computer Society, Pittsburgh, USA, pp. 306-307.

Alpern B, Auerbach J, Bala V, *et al.* (2005) A virtual execution environment for software deployment. In: Vitek J (ed.) The 1st ACM/Usenix Conference on Virtual Execution Environments. USENIX Association, Chicago, USA, pp. 175-183.

Ao G (2000) Software hot swapping techniques for upgrading mission-critical applications on the fly. Ph.D. thesis, Carleton University.

Armbrust M, Fox A, Griffith R, Joseph AD, Katz RH, Konwinski A, Lee G, Patterson DA, Rabkin A, Zaharia M (2009) Above the clouds: A Berkeley view of cloud computing. Tech. rep., UC Berkeley Reliable Adaptive Distributed Systems Laboratory, URL http://radlab.cs.berkeley.edu/.

Arnold RS (1994) Software reengineering: a quick history. Communications of the ACM, 37(5): 13-14.

Benatallah B, Sheng QZ, Dumas M (2003) The self-serve environment for Web services composition. IEEE Internet Computing, 7(1): 40-48.

Bidan C, Issarmy V, Saridakis T, Zarras A (1998) A dynamic reconfiguration service for CORBA. In: 4th IEEE International Conference on Configurable Distributed Systems. IEEE Computer Society, Annapolis, Maryland, USA.

Blanchet C, Mollon R, Deleage G (2006) Building an encrypted file system on the EGEE Grid: Application to protein sequence analysis. In: The 1st International Conference on Availability, Reliability and Security, 2006. ARES 2006, IEEE Computer Society, Vienna Austria, p. 7.

Boari M, Lodolo E, Monti S, Pasini S (2008) Middleware for automatic dynamic reconfiguration of context-driven services. Microprocess Microsyst, 32(3): 145-158.

Bollinger T (1999) Linux in practice: An overview of applications. IEEE Software, 16(1): 72-80.

Buyya R, Yeo CS, Venugopal S, Broberg J, Brandic I (2009) Cloud computing and emerging it platforms: Vision, hype and reality for delivering computing as the 5th utility. Future Gener Comput Syst, 25(6): 599-616.

Caromel D, di Costanzo A, Delbe C (2007) Peer-to-peer and fault-tolerance: Towards deployment-based technical services. Future Generation Computer Systems, 23(7): 879-887.

C'erin C, Koskas M (2005) Mining traces of large-scale systems. In: Distributed and Parallel Computing. Lecture Notes in Computer Science, pp. 132-138.

Chen L, Zhu Q, Agrawal G (2006) Supporting dynamic migration in tightly coupled grid applications. In: SC '06: Proceedings of the 2006 ACM/IEEE Conference on Supercomputing. ACM, New York, NY, USA, p. 117.

Chu L, Shen K, Tang H, Yang T, Zhou J (2005) Dependency isolation for threadbased multi-tier Internet services. In: Knightly E, Makki K (eds.) 24th Annual Joint Conference of the IEEE Computer and Communications Societies. IEEE Computer Society, Miami, USA, vol. 2, pp. 796-806.

Cochrane P (2001) Napster—just the beginning. Journal of the Institution of British Telecommunications Engineers, 2: 71-72.

Cohensive FT (2009) URL http://www.cohesiveft.com/.

Coles J (2005) The evolving grid deployment and operations model within EGEE, LCG and GRIDPP. In: Stockinger H (ed.) First International Conference on e-Science and Grid Computing, 2005. IEEE Computer Society, Melbourne Australia, pp. 90-97.

Dart S (1991) Concepts in configuration management systems. In: SCM '91: Proceedings of the 3rd International Workshop on Software Configuration Management. ACM, New York, NY, USA, pp. 1-18.

Dean J, Ghemawat S (2008) Mapreduce: Simplified data processing on large clusters. Communications of the ACM, 51:107-113.

Denneberg V, Fromm P (1998) Oscar: An open software concept for autonomous robots. In: Cook G, Kaynak O (eds.) The 24th Annual Conference of the IEEE Industrial Electronics Society, 1998. IEEE Computer Society, Aachen, Germany, Vol. 2, pp. 1192-1197.

Draper C, George R, Vitaletti M (2004) Installable unit deployment descriptor for autonomic solution management. In: Tjoa AM, Wagner RR (eds.) 15th International Workshop on Database and Expert Systems Applications, 2004. IEEE Computer Scociety, Los Alamitos, CA, USA, pp. 742-746

Dustdar S, Schreiner W (2005) A survey on Web services composition. Int J Web Grid Serv, 1(1): 1-30.

Elastra (2009) URL http://www.elastra.com/.

Estublier J (2000) Software configuration management: A roadmap. In: ICSE '00: Proceedings of the Conference on the Future of Software Engineering. ACM, New York, NY, USA, pp. 279-289.

Foster I, Kesselman C (1998) The Grid: Blueprint for a New Computing Infrastructure. Morgan Kaufmann Publishers, San Francisco, USA.

Foster I, Kesselman C, Tuecke S (2001) The anatomy of the grid: Enabling scalable virtual organizations. International Journal of High Performance Computing Applications, 15(3): 200-222.

Gagliardi F, Begin ME (2005) EGEE—providing a production quality grid for escience. In: Local to Global Data Interoperability—Challenges and Technologies, 2005. IEEE Computer Society, Sardinia, Italy, pp. 88-92.

Ghemawat S, Gobioff H, Leung ST (2003) The Google file system. SIGOPS Oper Syst Rev, 37(5): 29-43.

Goldberg RP (1976) Survey of virtual machine research. IEEE Computer Magazine, 7(6):34-35.

Gong Y, Dong F, Li W, Xu Z (2003) Vega infrastructure for resource discovery in grids. J Comput Sci Technol, 18(4): 413-422.

Grubb P, Takang AA (2004) Software Maintenance: Concepts and Practice. Publishing House of Electronics Industry, New Jersey, USA.

Sun H, Liu W, Wo T, Hu C (2006) Crown node server: An enhanced grid service container based on gt4 wsrf core. In: 5th International Conference on Grid and Cooperative Computing Workshops, 2006. IEEE Computer Society, Changsha, China, pp. 510-517.

Javadpour R (2001) A neural network approach to dependent reliability estimation. PhD thesis, Louisiana State university.

Jin H (2004) Chinagrid: Making grid computing a reality. In: Chen Z, Chen H, Miao Q, Fu Y, Fox E, Lim E (eds.) Digital Libraries: International Collaboration and Cross-Fertilization. Springer, Singapore, pp. 13-24.

Johnston WE, Gannon D, Nitzberg B (1999) Grids as production computing environments: The engineering aspects of NASA's information power grid. In: The 8th International Symposium on High Performance Distributed Computing, 1999. IEEE Computer Society, Redondo Beach, USA, pp. 197-204.

Kaavo (2009) URL http://www.kaavo.com/home.

Keahey K, Foster I, Freeman T, Zhang XH, Galron D (2005) Virtual workspaces in the grid. In: EuroPar'05: Euro-Par 2005 Parallel Processing. Lisbon, Portugal, pp. 421-431.

Konstantinou AV, Eilam T, Kalantar M, Totok AA, Arnold W, Snible E (2009) An architecture for virtual solution composition and deployment in infrastructure clouds. In: VTDC '09: Proceedings of the 3rd International Workshop on Virtualization Technologies in Distributed Computing. ACM, New York, NY, USA, pp. 9-18.

Kramer J, Magee J (1985) Dynamic configuration for distributed systems. IEEE Transaction on Software Engineering, 11(4): 424-436.

Kramer J, Magee J (1990) The evolving philosopher's problem: Dynamic change management. IEEE Transaction on Software Engineering, 16(11):1293-1306.

Liben-Nowell D, Balakrishnan H, Karger D (2002) Observations on the dynamic evolution of peer-to-peer networks. In: IPTPS '01: Revised Papers from the First International Workshop on Peer-to-Peer Systems. Springer-Verlag, London, UK, pp. 22-33.

Lientz BP, Swanson EB, Tompkins GE (1978) Characteristics of application software maintenance. Communications of the ACM, 21(6): 466-471.

Machida F, Kawato M, Maeno Y (2008) Just-in-time server provisioning using virtual machine standby and request prediction. In: ICAC '08: Proceedings of the 2008 International Conference on Autonomic Computing. IEEE Computer Society, Washington DC, USA, pp. 163-171.

Miguel L. Bote-Lorenzo, Yannis A Dimitriadis (2004) Grid characteristics and uses: A grid definition. In: Proceedings of the 2006 ACM/IEEE Conference on Supercomputing. Springer-Verlag, p. 288.

Mitsos Y, Andritsopoulos F, Kagklis D (2004) A study for provisioning of qos Web-based services to the end-user. In: SAC '04: Proceedings of the 2004 ACM symposium on applied computing. ACM, New York, NY, USA, pp. 318-321.

Moazami-Goudarzi K (1999) Consistency preserving dynamic reconfiguration of distributed systems. PhD thesis, Imperial College, London, UK.

Mugler J, Naughton T, Scott SL (2005) Oscar meta-package system. In: 19th International Symposium on High Performance Computing Systems and Applications, 2005. IEEE Computer Society, Guelph, Ontario, Canada, pp. 353-360.

Pellegrini NC (1999) Dynamic reconfiguration of CORBA-based applications. In: Mitchell R, Wills AC, Bosch Jan, Meyer B (eds.) Technology of Object-Oriented Languages and Systems, 1999. IEEE Computer Society, Los Alamitos, CA, USA, pp. 329-340.

Reed DA (2003) Grids, the teragrid and beyond. IEEE Computer, 36(1): 62-68.

Ripeanu M, Iamnitchi A, Foster I (2002) Mapping the gnutella network. IEEE Internet Computing, 6(1): 50-57.

Rusnak JJ (2005) The design structure analysis system—a tool to analyze software architecture. PhD thesis, Harvard University.

Sabharwal R (2006) Grid infrastructure deployment using smartfrog technology. In: Bader DA, Khokhar AA (eds.) International conference on Networking and Services, 2006. IEEE Computer Society, Washington DC, USA, p. 73.

Sangal N, Jordan E, Sinha V, et al. (2005) Using dependency models to manage complex software architecture. In: Gabriel RP (ed.) International Conference on Object Oriented Programming, Systems, Languages and Applications, 2005. IEEE Computer Society, San Diego, USA, pp. 167-176.

Shwartz L, Ayachitula N, Maheswaran S, Grabarnik G (2005) Managing system capabilities and requirements using rough set theory. Research Report RC23699, IBM.

Smith E, Anderson P (2004) Dynamic reconfiguration for grid fabrics. In: Buyya R (ed.) 5th IEEE/ACM International Workshop on Grid Computing. IEEE Computer Society, Pittsburgh, USA, pp. 86-93.

Smith M, Friese T, Freisleben B (2004) Towards a service-oriented ad hoc grid. In: 3rd International Workshop on Parallel and Distributed Computing, 2004. Third International Symposium on/Algorithms, Models and Tools for Parallel Computing on Heterogeneous Networks, 2004. IEEE Computer Society, Cork, Ireland, pp. 201-208.

Stein S, Jennings NR, Payne TR (2007) Provisioning heterogeneous and unreliable providers for service workflows. In: AAMAS '07: Proceedings of the 6th International Joint Conference on Autonomous Agents and Multiagent Systems. ACM, New York, NY, USA, pp. 1-3.

Stein S, Jennings NR, Payne TR (2008) Flexible service provisioning with advance agreements. In: AAMAS '08: Proceedings of the 7th International Joint Conference on Autonomous Agents and Multiagent Systems. International Foundation for Autonomous Agents and Multiagent Systems, Richland, SC, pp. 249-256.

Tingey A (1998) NT vs. solaris x86. Computer Graphics World, 21(11): 8.

Tolksdorf R (2002) A dependency markup language for Web services. In: Chaudhr A, Jeckle M, Rahm E, Unland R (eds.) Web and Database-Related Workshops on Web, Web Services, and Database Systems. Springer, London, UK, pp. 129-140.

Urgaonkar B, Shenoy P, Chandra A, Goyal P, Wood T (2008) Agile dynamic provisioning of multi-tier Internet applications. ACM Trans Auton Adapt Syst, 3(1): 1-39.

Villela D, Pradhan P, Rubenstein D (2007) Provisioning servers in the application tier for e-commerce systems. ACM Trans Internet Technol, 7(1): 7.

Wei XH, Li WW, Tatebe O, Xu GC, Hu L, Ju JB (2005) Integrating local job scheduler - lsfTMwith gfarmTM, pp. 196-204.

Wikipedia Provisioning (2002) URL http://en.wikipedia.org/wiki/Provisioning.

Yang H, Xu Z, Sun Y, Zheng Q (2005) Modeling and performanceanalysis of the vega grid system. In: E-SCIENCE '05: Proceedings of the First International Conference on e-Science and Grid Computing. IEEE Computer Society, Washington DC, USA, pp. 296-303.

Zielinski K, Jarzab M, Kosinski J (2005) Role of n_1 technology in the next generation grids middleware. In: Sloot PM, Hoekstra AG, Priol T, Reinefeld A, Bubak M (eds.) Advances in Grid Computing—EGC 2005. Springer, Amsterdam, The Netherlands, pp. 942-951.

2

Grid and Distributed Systems

Abstract: Grid computing is becoming more and more attractive for coordinating large-scale heterogeneous resource sharing and problem solving. Of particular interest for effective grid, computing is a software provisioning mechanism. To efficiently maintain and provision software upon a grid infrastructure, the middleware employed to manage the system is greatly important. Thus, understanding the principles and logic of grid middleware is the first step in designing the provisioning and maintenance system.

2.1 Fundamental Concepts

A grid is an Internet-connected computing environment in which computing and data resources are geographically distributed in different administrative domains, often with separate policies for security and resource use. With the introduction of OGSA, the focus of grid computing moved from legacy computing-intensive applications to service-oriented computing based on open standards. Nowadays, grids enable the sharing, discovery, selection and aggregation of distributed heterogeneous resources (i.e., computers, databases, visualization devices, scientific instruments and so forth). Accordingly, these grids have been proposed as the computing platform and global cyber-infrastructure for solving large-scale problems in science, engineering and business. Several countries and regions have established different grid backbones at national level. Examples include TeraGrid (Reed, 2003), Grid 5000 (Caromel *et al.*, 2007), D-Grid (Fieseler and Gürich, 2008), ChinaGrid (Jin, 2004), CNGrid (Gong *et al.*, 2003) and so forth.

In order to provide users with a seamless computing environment, grid middleware systems need to solve several challenges originating from the inherent features of the grid. One of the main challenges is the heterogeneity, which results from the multiplicity of heterogeneous resources and the vast range of technologies encompassed by the grid. Another challenge involves the multiple administrative domains and autonomy issues because of geographically distributed grid resources across multiple administrative domains and owned by different organizations. Other challenges include scalability (the problem of performance degradation as the size of grids increases) and dynamicity/adaptability (the problem of resource failing is high). Middleware systems must tailor their behavior dynamically and use the available resources and services efficiently and effectively.

2.2   The Principles of Grids

Before constructing a production level grid, we should understand the principles of grid technologies.

2.2.1   *Service-Oriented Architecture*

To efficiently and effectively support grid computing, and to express the business models easily, designers, developers and administrators need a group of Web service technologies to construct a real, user-friendly and content-rich set of applications. As a major trend in the Internet communication mechanism, service-oriented architecture (SOA) has been widely adopted as the fundamental protocol by many distributed systems, especially by the grid systems.

The goal of an SOA is to compose together fairly large chunks of functionality to form some service-oriented applications which are almost entirely built from existing software services. SOA used a collection of open standards (i) to wrap the components in a different localized runtime environment, (ii) to enable different clients including pervasive devices free access, and (iii) to reuse the existing components to compose more services. This feature significantly reduces the development costs and helps designers and developers concentrate more on business models and their internal logic rather than what underlies the systems.

SOAs use several communication standards based on XML to enhance the interoperability among application systems. As the atomic access point inside an SOA, the Web services are formally defined by three kernel standards: Web Service Description Language (WSDL), Simple Object Access Protocol (SOAP) and Universal Description Discovery and Integration (UDDI). Normally the functional interfaces and parameters of specific services are described using WSDL. The exchange of messages among Web services are encoded in the SOAP messaging framework and transported over HTTP or other Internet protocols (SMTP, FTP and so forth). A typical Web service lifecycle envisions the following scenario: A service provider publishes the WSDL description of their service in a UDDI, a registry that permits UDDI of Web services. Subsequently, service requesters can inspect the UDDI and locate/discover Web services that are of interest. Using the information provided by the WSDL description they can directly invoke the corresponding Web services. Furthermore, several Web services can be composed to achieve more complex functionality. All the invocation procedures are similar to remote procedure call (RPC) except the communications and deployments are described in the open standards.

Moreover, the open standards organizations such as W3C, OASIS and DMTF contribute many higher level standards to help different users construct their reusable, interoperable and discoverable services and applications. Some of these standards were widely adopted to construct grid and cloud systems, such as Web Services Resources Framework (WSRF), Web Services Security (WS-Security), Web Services Policy (WS-Policy) and so on.

2.2.2 Open Grid Service Architecture

As one of the most important principles, the Open Grid Service Architecture (OGSA) documents include the following descriptions:

• An architectural process which is maintained by the Open Grid Forum OGSA working group.

• A set of specifications and profiles that explain how to construct the hardware and software in a principal way.

• The essential software components that follow OGSA specifications and profiles.

To meet the requirements of distributed computing, OGSA also describes a set of system services. These services as follows have been widely implemented by several organizations and groups.

• *Infrastructure Services* are in charge of connecting the computing or storage resources and making these resources accessible in a secure approach. The majority of implementations of dynamic maintenance are inside these services. Normally these services are transparent to end users.

• *Execution Management Services* are mainly coordinating and dispatching job requests to the target computing resources according to end users' demands.

• *Data Services* are essential components of a grid to handle the transfers of files among the resources, the replicas and lifecycle of grid data.

• *Resource Management Services* provide appropriate tools to allow both resource users and owners to share the resources more efficiently and effectively. The content discussed in Chapter 7 will detail the enhancement of resource management services.

• *Security Services* inside the OGSA provide the authorization and authentication frameworks to guarantee the accessibility of resources securely.

• *Self-Management Services* charge the management and maintenance of grid's system services.

• *Information Services* in a grid are designed to manage the dynamic data or the events used for status monitoring, relatively static data used for discovery and any data that is logged.

2.3   Grid Middleware

Grid middleware is the kernel of grid system that is implemented to compose geographically distributed software and hardware resources. By facilitating different interfaces, application developers can design the desktop or Web-oriented applications in the grid style, normal users can submit their jobs to computing resources and grid administrators can easily and efficiently manage thousands of resources. In this section, we introduce the popular grid middleware that is equipped by global grid systems.

2.3.1   *Globus Toolkit*

The Globus project, funded by Globus Alliance[1], is an open source software toolkit to help different domain users construct the grid applications. Currently, majority grids (e.g. TeraGrid, LCG and so forth) facilitate Globus Toolkit (GT) solely or partially to construct their distributed infrastructure. The management units include computing power, databases and other tools. By composing these units, GT makes them secure online across virtual organizations without sacrificing local autonomy. As shown in Fig. 2.1, GT architecture has three main groups of services upon a security layer.

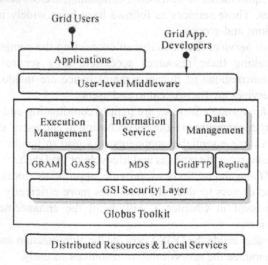

Fig. 2.1.   The software modules of Globus

•   *GSI Security Layer* (Welch, 2004) is the fundamental security infrastructure to support the authentication of grid users and a secure communication. It is

---

[1]   http://www.globus.org

implemented based on a series of protocols such as Secure Sockets Layer (SSL), Public Key Infrastructure (PKI) and X.509 Certificate Architecture. Basically, the GSI provides the following functions: single sign-on by user certificates, resource authentication by host certificates, communication encryption, authorization among users and delegation of authority and trust through proxies and certificate chain of trust for Certificate Authorities (CAs).

• *Execution Management* enables resource allocation through job submission, staging of executable files, job monitoring and result gathering. The kernel of resource management includes Globus Resource Allocation Manager (GRAM) (Czajkowski *et al.*, 1998). GRAM is a remote execution coordinator which periodically reports status during the course of the execution. Normally, a grid user requests a job submission described to the service containers on the remote host. After authentication and authorization checking, the GRAM service activates a job manager instance to orchestrate and monitor the status of execution. Conveniently, GRAM supports several local schedulers such as PBS (Henderson, 1995), LSF (Costen *et al.*, 1999; Wei *et al.*, 2005) and LoadLeveler (Skovira *et al.*, 1996). The job details are specified through the Globus Resource Specification Language (RSL), which is a part of GRAM. RSL provides syntax consisting of the attribute-value pairs for describing resources required for a job including the minimum memory and the number of CPUs.

• *Information Service* provide static and dynamic properties of the nodes that are connected to the grid. The kernel service inside Globus is the Monitoring and Discovery Service (MDS) (Laszewski *et al.*, 1997). MDS supports the publishing and querying of resource information. MDS is designed in a three-tier structure. The bottom layer includes a set of Information Providers (IPs) that collect the properties and status of resources. Furthermore, in the second tier, the Grid Resource Information Service (GRIS) is a single daemon that responds to queries about the resource properties and updates its cache at intervals defined by the time-to-live (TTL) by querying the relevant IPs. In the top level, the Grid Information Index Service (GIIS) indexes the resource information provided by other GRIS and GIIS that are registered with it. The standard set of IPs provides data on CPU type, system architecture, number of processors and memory available, among others.

• *Data Management* is a set of utilities and libraries for transmitting, storing and managing massive data sets that are part of many scientific computing applications (Allcock *et al.*, 2001). Data Management consists of two components as follows:

- GridFTP (Allcock *et al.*, 2004) is an extension of the standard FTP protocol that provides secure, efficient and reliable data movements in a grid. Otherwise, GridFTP provides GSI support for authenticated data transfer, third-party transfer invocation and striped, parallel and partial data transfer support.

- Replica supports multiple caches for a file throughout the lifecycle. By registering with Replica Location Service (RLS), a file and its replicas can be automatically created and deleted according to proper strategies. Within RLS, each file is identified by its Logical File Name (LFN) and is registered within a logical collection. The record for a file points to its physical locations. This information is available from the RLS upon querying.

2.3.2   *CGSP*

ChinaGrid Support Platform (CGSP) integrates all sorts of heterogeneous resources, especially education and research resources distributed over China Education and Research Network (CERNET), to provide transparent and convenient grid services for scientific research and higher education. The core work in this book centers around the CGSP middleware. In moving towards its destination, CGSP is developed based on the following motivations:

• To provide a platform for a grid to construct from the top portal to the integration of the bottom resources of the grid. Besides the uniform management of heterogeneous resources, it provides the capability for portal building, job defining, application packaging and grid monitoring.

• To support the secondary development of grid services to provide the flexibility of the system. The middleware should provide the parallel programming interface and its running environment which support the complicated development in a grid.

• To follow the latest grid standard and integrate existing advanced technology to enhance reusability and interoperability.

• To provide an extensible and reconfigurable grid framework, in order to meet the purpose of ChinaGrid to cover top universities of China in the near future, and satisfy the autonomy of each ChinaGrid application or unit.

• To avoid unnecessary data delivery over the grids. It means that the data required by the computing job do not stream with the job description file. Instead, they are delivered to a virtual data space in a data manager first. Subsequently, the computing nodes can access the data directly when the job begins to be executed.

To support the aforementioned motivations, the CGSP middleware consists of the following essential modules as shown in Fig. 2.2.

• *Service Container* (Qi *et al.*, 2007) builds a basic environment for the installation, deployment, running and monitoring of CGSP services and other application services in each computing node. It is definitely a fundamental runtime environment for the grid services and supplies "service-oriented facilities for computing" to shield the heterogeneity of different operating systems. Although it expands from GT4, it enhances the hot deploy mechanism and the remote deploy functions to support the dynamic management for grid applications.

• *Security Manager* (Wang, 2006) focuses on user identity authentication, identity mapping, service and resource authorization and secure message passing between grid nodes.

• *Information Center* (Zhang *et al.*, 2006) provides the service registration, publishing, metadata management, service querying, service matching and resources status collection for the grid services in a uniform way. Furthermore, it provides an extendable model mechanism like Common Information Model (CIM) to support various types of resources. Examples include computers, instruments, clusters and mainframes.

• *Data Manager* (Wu S *et al.*, 2007a) is designed to shield the heterogeneous underlying of the storage resources through a uniform data transferring protocol. In addition, it provides a uniform storage resource access model.

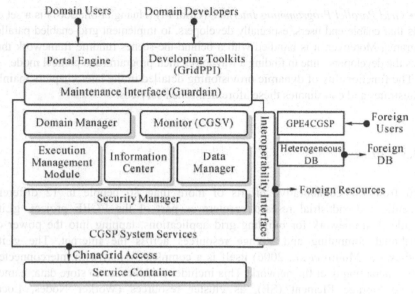

Fig. 2.2. The architecture of CGSP

• *Execution Management Module* (Ma *et al.*, 2006; 2008) is one of the most complicated kernel modules of CGSP. It accepts requests from end users in the form of an SOAP message, and then interacts with the Information Center to adopt relevant services according to the job descriptions. Meanwhile, it supports the work flow. Furthermore, it is in charge of the process control of the work flow job, including parsing and compiling a work flow description file named Grid Job Description Language (GJDL) which is extended from the Business Process Execution Language (BPEL) protocol (Cao *et al.*, 2006). Otherwise, it supports the invocation of the legacy job by using General Running Service (GRS) (Liu *et al.*, 2006) which is used to pack the legacy object codes running on different operating systems.

• *Heterogeneous Database* (HDB) (Li *et al.*, 2008) aims to enable end users access the services provided by various heterogeneous databases in a grid. It provides unified accessing methods which make the data integration possible. Hence, HDB is capable of being a unified accessing point for the large-scale data stored in the heterogeneous databases.

• *Domain Manager* is in charge of user management, logging and accounting and user identity mapping between different grid domains.

• *Monitor (CGSV)* (Wu Y *et al.*, 2007) mainly focuses on monitoring of the load of grid resources, quality of services, user actions, job status and network. It ensures the applications are running correctly. In CGSP's implementation, we name it as ChinaGrid SuperVision (CGSV).

• *Portal Engine* provides a Web-oriented approach to access the services of ChinaGrid. It is also a convenient and public access point for the customized grid applications.

• *Grid Parallel Programming Interface* (GridPPI) (Huang *et al.*, 2007) is a set of APIs that enable end users, especially developers, to implement grid-enabled parallel programs. Moreover, it is bundled with a behind-the-scenes runtime framework that saves the developers' time in finding a way to run their programs in a parallel mode.

The functionality of dynamic provisioning detailed in the later chapters mainly orchestrates and coordinates these aforementioned services.

2.3.3   gLite

Born from the collaborative efforts of more than 80 people in 12 different academic and industrial research centers as part of the EGEE project, gLite provides a framework for building grid applications, tapping into the power of distributed computing and storage resources across the Internet. The gLite middleware (Munro *et al.*, 2006) itself is a complex system with interconnected parts, interacting over the network. This includes middleware to store data, named dCache Storage Element (SE), as cluster resources (Worker Nodes, Local Resource Management System and NFS server). Every gLite instance has Computing Element (CE) as a front-end for job submission. Information Service (IS) (or "site BDII") provides information about the grid resources and their status which can be used for monitoring and accounting. Current gLite implementation uses Globus MDS for resource discovery and to publish the resource status.

As shown in Fig. 2.3, the gLite middleware consists of several components distributed in the server and client layers.

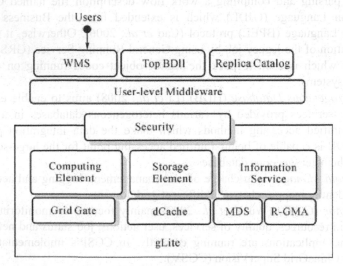

Fig. 2.3. The architecture of gLite

• *Security* in gLite provides the authentications and authorizations in terms of virtual organizations. A user must join a VO supported by the infrastructure running gLite to be authenticated and authorized to use grid resources. Partially relying on GT, the GSI in LCG and EGEE enables secure authentication and communication over the Internet. Specifically, GSI is based on public key encryption, X.509 certificates and the SSL communication protocol, with extensions for single sign-on and delegation.

• *User-Level Middleware* is the access point to the gLite grid in the form of user interfaces. This can be any machine where end users have a personal account and where their user certificates are installed. From a graphic application, a user can be authenticated and authorized to use the LCG and EGEE resources, and can access the functionalities offered by the Information, Workload and Data Management Systems. It provides CLI tools to perform some basic grid operations as follows:
  - List all the resources suitable to execute a given job;
  - Submit jobs for execution;
  - Cancel jobs;
  - Retrieve the output of finished jobs;
  - Show the status of submitted jobs;
  - Retrieve the logging and bookkeeping information of jobs;
  - Copy, replicate and delete files from the grid;
  - Retrieve the status of different resources from the Information System.

• *Computing Element* (CE) is a set of computing resources localized at a site (i.e., a cluster, a computing farm). A CE includes a Grid Gate (GG), which acts as a generic interface to the cluster; a Local Resource Management System (LRMS, sometimes called batch system), the cluster itself, a collection of Worker Nodes, and the nodes where the jobs are run.

• *Storage Element* (SE) (Kunszt et al., 2005) provides uniform access to data storage resources. The SE may control simple disk servers, large disk arrays or tape-based Mass Storage Systems (MSS). The majority of LCG/EGEE sites provide at least one SE. The Storage Resource Manager/dCache Storage System is a data management system, which has been successfully in use in high energy physics and as a grid storage element for many years. It is a disk pool management system for data distributed on many servers and disks. It consists of a dCache server and one or several pool nodes. The server executes data access management and system administration. The pool nodes serve the disks and provide the storage. In large installations it is also possible to distribute the management and administration tasks on several servers.

SE can support different data access protocols and interfaces. By default, GSI-FTP is the protocol for whole-file transfers.

• *Workload Management System* (WMS) (Marco et al., 2009) distributed in the client layer is to accept user jobs, to assign them to the most appropriate Computing Element (CE), to record their status and retrieve their output. The resource broker is the machine where the WMS services run.

The Job Description Language (JDL) is designed to describe the jobs submitted from users. It specifies which service to run, and its parameters, files to be moved to and from the worker node on which the job is run, input grid files needed and any requirements on the CE and the Worker Node.

2.3.4 *UNICORE*

UNICORE (Erwin, 2002) is a vertically integrated grid computing environment that facilitates the following:

• A seamless, secure and intuitive access to resources in a distributed environment for end users.

• Solid authentication mechanisms integrated into their administration procedures, to reduce training effort and support requirements for grid sites.

• Easy relocation of computer jobs to different platforms for both end users and grid sites.

As the kernel middleware of the D-Grid in Germany, UNICORE is constructed in a three-tier architecture (Fig. 2.4). These tiers include (i) the client tier which runs on a Java enabled user workstation or a PC, (ii) a gateway and (iii) several instances of Network Job Supervisors (NJS) that are deployed on distributed servers and multiple instances of Target System Interfaces (TSI) executing on different nodes that provide interfaces to the underlying local resource management systems, such as operating systems and batch subsystems. The functions of these components are depicted as follows:

• *User Tier* consists of the applications that run on a user's personal computer or a local workstation or PC.

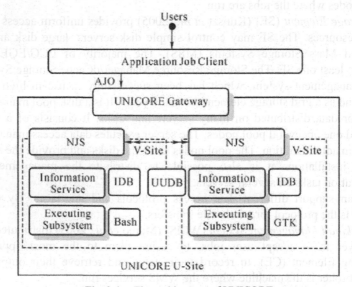

Fig. 2.4.   The architecture of UNICORE

• *Server Tier* is on the top level, each participating computer center defines one or several UNICORE sites (U-Sites).

• *Target System Tier* is the access point provided by a U-Site for UNICORE computing or data resources. They are organized as one or several virtual sites (V-Sites) which can represent the execution and/or storage systems at the computer centers.

More specifically, the components inside different tiers are listed as follows:

• *Application Job Client* is a graphical interface that assists the domain users to create interdependent jobs or composite jobs (e.g. work flow jobs) that can be executed on any UNICORE site transparently.

- Plug-enabled Manner: Since scientists and engineers use specific scientific applications, the user interface is built in a plug-enabled manner in order to extend it with plug-ins that allows them to prepare specific application input.

- Work Flow: A user job can be described as a set of one or more directed acyclic graphs.

• *Gateway* provides a set of principle services to handle interactions with security, job management and resource management.

- Security: Single sign-on function through X.509v3 certificates to all registered users.

- Resource Management: Users select the target system and specify the required resources. The UNICORE client verifies the correctness of jobs and alerts users to correct errors immediately.

- Data Management: Handles the staging data related to users' jobs among computing nodes and UNICORE's U-Space (storage service available for a job) during the lifecycle of a job. In addition to the staging data, it also charges the inter-operation among different U-Spaces. All the transferring works are executed in a transparent way.

- Job Management: It is in charge of interaction with the application job clients to orchestrate the user's job requests to target computing resources.

• *V-Site* is one of the essential components of UNICORE that wraps the heterogeneous computing resources as the common target system. The kernel services provided by V-Site include:

- Executing Subsystem: It is in charge of execution of jobs from gateway's orchestration. It supports legacy jobs which might be traditional batch processing by allowing users to include their old job scripts as part of a UNICORE job.

- Information Service: It is implemented by means of an Incarnation Database (IDB) that records the details of resources. By interacting with UNICORE User Database (UUDB), the IDB distributed in different V-Sites can interact to complete complicated jobs.

2.3.5 *ProActive*

As the important constructing component of Grid 5000, the ProActive (Baduel *et al.*, 2006) is much more like a programming model instead of a middleware. Here its internal working procedure shown in Fig. 2.5 focuses on a running scenario. The running environment of ProActive is a Java Virtual Machine (JVM) deployed on distributed computing resources or virtual machines.

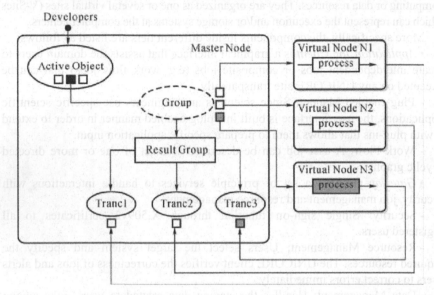

Fig. 2.5.   The running scenario of ProActive

• *Active Object*: As shown in Fig. 2.5, applications built using ProActive consists of a number of entities named active objects. Each active object has one distinguished element, defined as the root, that uniquely refers to the active object. In addition, each active object has its own thread of control and is allowed to identify in what order to serve the incoming method requests. These active objects can be created remotely by a master node and coordinated in an asynchronous approach to complete complicated jobs.

• *Group*: The group object is a kind of mechanism provided by ProActive to achieve an asynchronous remote method invocation for a group of remote objects. The elements can be included in a typed group only if their class equals or extends the class specified at the group creation. A method invocation of a group object will asynchronously be propagated to all members of the group using multi-threading.

• *Result Group*: The result group is transparently built at the invocation time of the normal group, with a future for each elementary reply. It will be dynamically updated with the incoming results in different tranches, thus gathering results. Thereby, the result group is a special group that charges data collections.

• *Virtual Nodes*: The virtual nodes defined in ProActive consist of the actual executing unit that is normally identified as a simple string name. The node list is defined in a deployment descriptor. During the runtime, each virtual node can be mapped into one or a set of actual ProActive Nodes. Thus, a virtual node is a concept of a distributed program or component, while a node is actually a deployment concept: it is an object that lives in a JVM, hosting active objects.

2.4 Dynamic Provisioning in Middleware

In this section, we will discuss the facilitation of dynamic provisioning technologies for deploying grid middleware and user applications.

As mentioned in Section 1.2, we classify the provisioning activities into two layers. The server provisioning will concentrate on deploying and maintaining system level stuff such as networking, the operating system and middleware. On the other hand, the user provisioning simply charges the management of application services. Hereby, we conclude the provisioning targets in the following sections.

2.4.1 Provisioning of Middleware

A comparison of the various middleware systems based on their architecture, implementation technologies and system services is given in Table 2.1.

Table 2.1 Provisioning of middleware

		Globus	CGSP	gLite	UNICORE	ProActive
Grid		TeraGrid	ChinaGrid	EGEE, LCG	D-Grid	Grid5000
Region		United States	P.R.China	Europe	Germany	France
Tech.		Java, C++	Java	C++	Java, C++	Java
Arch.		SOA, WSRF	SOA, WSRF	SOA	SOA, WSRF	RMI
API		MPICH	GridPPI	gLite API	Job client, HiLA	PA Classes
System Services	Infra.	Container	HAND Services	N/A	N/A	N/A
	Self Man.	VWS	Guardian Services	LRMS	N/A	PADeploy
	Info.	MDS	Info. Service, CGSV	MDS, R-GMA	IDB, UUDB	N/A
	Exec. Man.	GRAM	GRS, BPEL	CE, LRMS	NJS	AO/Group
	Data Man.	GridFTP, RLS	Data Manager, HDB, GridFTP	SE	U-Space	SSL
	Security	GSI	GSI, Domain Services	GSI	X509	SSH

It is not hard to conclude that each middleware consists of a set of system services which charge different functions defined in OGSA specification. Here the actual provisioning process of middleware is to maintain the atomic services in distributed environments.

2.4.2   *Provisioning Using Middleware*

In practice, the normal users of a grid hardly have the privilege to provision system services due to different security policies. Sequentially, most users are more concerned about how to use middleware services to construct their applications.

As depicted in Table 2.1, some middleware (e.g. Globus, CGSP and ProActive) provides the provisioning functions in the infrastructure and self-management services. The advantage of provision user applications by facilitating middleware is obvious.

• Users can construct their services in the meantime without complicated requests to the administrator of grids.

• The scale and size of computing resources for user applications can be allocated dynamically.

• The isolation of server provisioning can enhance the security of a grid infrastructure.

In Chapters 5, 6 and 7, we will demonstrate how to complete provisioning operations using middleware.

2.5   ChinaGrid and Related Projects

ChinaGrid (Jin, 2004), funded by the Ministry of Education in China, is an open scientific discovery infrastructure combining the leadership class resources of 22 top universities in China to create an integrated, persistent computational resource. Connected by high-performance CERNET, ChinaGrid integrates high-performance computers, data resources and tools and high-end experimental facilities.

Currently, ChinaGrid provides more than 20 teraflops of computing power and over 200 terabytes of online and archival data storage capacity. Researchers can freely access these resources from the member universities. With this combination of resources, ChinaGrid is the most comprehensive distributed infrastructure for open scientific research in China.

Since the majority of the material in this book was completed on the ChinaGrid project, this section introduces the optional components (e.g. CGSV and GPE4CGSP as shown in Fig. 2.6) and the applications grid inside ChinaGrid.

2.5.1   CGSV

ChinaGrid SuperVision (CGSV) (Wu *et al.*, 2007; 2010) sponsored by HP, is the program launched to handle monitoring-related issues for the ChinaGrid project. In accordance with the latest efforts in SOA and grid communities, CGSV seeks a set of resource measurement and control services for the operation of ChinaGrid ecology.

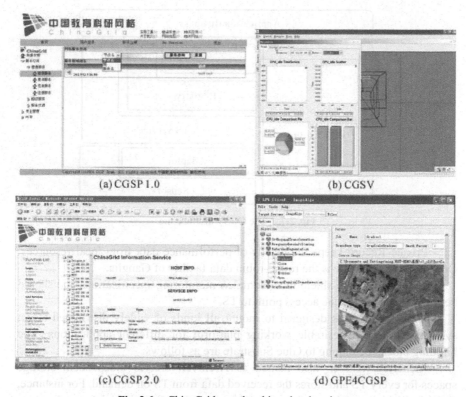

        (a) CGSP 1.0   (b) CGSV

        (c) CGSP 2.0   (d) GPE4CGSP

Fig. 2.6. ChinaGrid portal and its related projects

The primary idea of grid monitoring is to integrate heterogeneous monitoring deployments or facilities of grid participants. Accordingly, a hierarchical structure is employed as follows:

- At resource level, details of performance data are collected and stored by virtue of any methods;

- Heterogeneous monitoring can be glued/integrated into the substrate of CGSV;

- Only useful data required by the applications are extracted from resources. These data will be archived for later use. Fig. 2.7 shows the logic components of CGSV. Based on the above philosophy, we have the following terms for the CGSV case.

• *Target System (TS)* refers to integrated objects or a close bundle of monitored resources. Some WSDM-compliant services are constructed to export monitoring-related data on behalf of TS. Usually, the components deployed on TS are objects as follows:

- Sensors are the actual entity to collect performance data;

- Adaptor is used to interoperate with third-party monitoring tools;

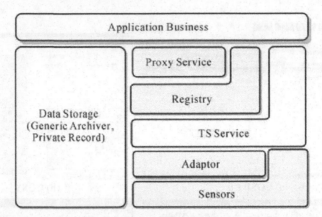

Fig. 2.7.   The CGSV architecture

- Private Record keeps the details of performance data from local resources. One conceptive sample is the round-robin data facility of Ganglia.

- TS Service try to shield local complex monitoring specifications and should be regarded as the unique access point to TS.

• *Glue Substrate* is designed to mount all kinds of widely distributed target systems to form a desirable working platform for different applications. The building blocks belonging to Glue Substrate are as follows:

- Generic Archiver, also named as Archiver, creates independent storage spaces for every TS and stores the received data from TS on demand. For instance, Generic Archiver needs not understand the semantics of received data in advance;

- Registry maintains the metadata of TS and other components (e.g. Archivers and Proxy Services);

- Proxy Service makes data retrieval from a substrate or TS, which will save much effort for application developers.

• *Application Business* in CGSV is the generic name for the modules that work on plain performance data of resources, such as Visualization and Depot for grid accounting.

2.5.2   *GPE4CGSP*

GPE4CGSP(Wu Y *et al.*, 2006; Wu S *et al.*, 2007b), funded by Intel, is an interactive module that coordinates the job requests between ChinaGrid underlying resources and those distributed in the alien grids. GPE4CGSP is implemented on Intel's Grid Programming Environment (GPE) framework.

GPE works in a three-layer architecture as shown in Fig. 2.8.

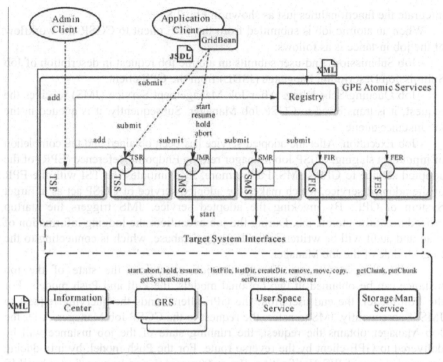

Fig. 2.8. The architecture of GPE4CGSP

• *Target System Interfaces Layer* is implemented as the BaseTSI and RemoteTSI in gpe4gtk. These are the bottommost interfaces for the target systems. Nearly all of the interfaces are atomic and independent of each other.

• *Service (Resource) Logic Layer* is designed to handle the basic logic of GPE's atomic services. All of the services (resources) are tightly coupled. These services will generate an instance of *Target System Resources* (TSR) when adding a Target System (TSS). Similarly, they will create an instance of Job Management Resource (JMR) when submitting a new JSDL job. Sequentially, an instance of Storage Management Resource (SMR) will be initiated to proceed the staging files. Meanwhile, the instances of File Import Resource (FIR) and File Export Resource (FER) are generated to handle the status monitoring during a job's execution. JMR will accept the control messages from the client side and deliver it to the target system.

• *Client Layer* is a graphical user interface enhanced with GridBean technologies. It consists of admin clients and application clients. The admin clients mainly communicate with the Target System Factory (TSF) and Registry Service (RS) to manage and provision the target systems. On the other hand, the application clients communicate with Grid Bean Service (GBS), RS, TSS and JMS to finish the controlling for the GPE's job processing.

The implementation of GPE4CGSP focuses on the Target System Interface (TSI). We call CgspTSI which communicates with the system services of CGSP to integrate the functionalities just as shown in Fig. 2.8.

When an atomic job is submitted from the GPE client to CGSP, the workflow of the job instance is as follows:

- Job Submission. End-user submits an atomic job request in description of Job Submission Description Language (JSDL) from the GPE client.

- Job Queuing/Scheduling. After Job Management Service (JMS) receives the request, it is transferred to CGSP Job Manager. Subsequently, it is queued in the job instance queue.

- Job Execution. After the adopted service has been obtained and the completion of input data staging, CGSP Job Manager returns Endpoint Reference (EPR) of the adopted service to GPE's JMS. Furthermore, JMS initiates the TSI with the EPR of the adopted service, which makes the adopted service of CGSP act as a Target System of GPE. By invoking the adopted service, JMS triggers the startup procedure of the atomic job. During the job execution, the logging information of state and audit will be written in the logging database, which is connecting to the Log Module of the Job Manager.

- Controlling/Monitoring. During the job execution, the state of the job instance can be obtained in two optional models, the Pull and Push models. For the Pull model, the end user from the GPE client sends the querying request to JMS. Subsequently, JMS transfers the request to the CGSP Job Manager. After the Job Manager obtains the request, the running state of the job instance will be delivered to GPE client by the reverse route. For the Push model, by introducing the mechanism of WS-Notification, the state message can be transferred by JMS from Job Manager directly to GPE client. Meanwhile, the end-user form GPE client can carry out some controlling operations to the job instance by sending the controlling messages.

- Job Result. Once the atomic job instance is completed successfully, Job Manager will invoke the Data Management of CGSP to transfer the job result from the adopted service to the end-user's virtual space in GPE.

2.5.3   *Application Grids*

There are five application grids that have been implemented upon CGSP grid middleware. Different from the bottom middleware, the application grids concentrate the working flow in different domains and are dedicated to making domain experts work on ChinaGrid conveniently. The five application grids are the bioinformatics grid, image grid, course online grid, MDPGrid and CFD grid, respectively.

The bioinformatics grid integrates heterogeneous large-scale computing and storage facilities within ChinaGrid to provide bioinformatics supercomputing services for bioinformatics researchers through the Web interface, which is very user-friendly. There are three key modules in the bioinformatics grid. They are: (i) Management of Heterogeneous Resources; (ii) Monitoring; (iii) Integration of

Heterogeneous Bioinformatics Computing Tools.

The image grid is a grid image-processing platform based on ChinaGrid infrastructure, which is an integrated environment hiding inner heterogeneous resources and dynamic information. It not only realizes cooperative characteristics, but also affords a secure and transparent image-processing environment with correlative services. The remarkable characteristics of the image-processing platform are application development, runtime environment and remote visualization.

MDPGrid includes three data intensive grid applications, High Energy Physics Computing, Alpha Magnetic Spectrometer (AMS) Experiment and University Digital Museums. High Energy Physics Computing, based on MDPGrid, is a solution for the processing and analyzing of the massive data. The AMS Experiment Project is a large-scale physics experiment on the International Space Station (ISS), with the main purpose of looking for antimatter in the universe, searching for the source of dark matter and measuring the source of cosmic rays. The University Digital Museum Grid (UDMGrid) is for integrating the enormous dispersed resources of various digital museums, to share the resources effectively and eliminate the information island, to filter and classify the collections information and to provide an appropriate information service to users according to their knowledge levels and motivation, through a unified grid portal.

The Computational Fluid Dynamics (CFD) grid provides the infrastructure to access different CFD applications across different physical domains and security firewalls. By defining a standard CFD workflow and general interfaces for exchanging mesh data, the platform facilitates interoperating between CFD applications.

The Course Online Grid (realcourse in short) is a video stream service supported by a collection of physical servers distributed all over China. The 3,000+ hours of videos are from different universities within ChinaGrid.

2.6 Summary

In this chapter, we discussed the detailed definitions in the principle standard, OGSA, and introduced five grid middlewares that have been used to construct popular grid testbeds in the world. By exploring their kernel mechanisms and components, we compared the convenience of constructing application grids and their difficulties for provisioning. Later in this chapter, we detailed the ChinaGrid which is the fundamental environment for the material in this book. Understanding the principles and motivations of ChinaGrid and its related projects can help readers grasp basic concepts that will be discussed in the later chapters.

References

Allcock B, Bester J, Bresnahan J, Chervenak AL, Kesselman C, Meder S, Nefedova V, Quesnel D, Tuecke S, Foster I (2001) Secure, efficient data transport and replica management for high-performance data-intensive computing. In: MSS '01: Proceedings of the 18th IEEE Symposium on Mass Storage Systems and Technologies. IEEE Computer Society, Washington, DC, USA, p. 13.

Allcock W, Foster I, Madduri R (2004) Reliable data transport: A critical service for the grid. In: Building Service Based Grid Workshop, GGF11. Honolulu's Haiaii, USA.

Baduel L, Baude F, Caromel D, Contes A, Huet F, Morel M, Quilici R (2006) Programming, deploying, composing for the Grid. In: Cunha JC, Rana OF (eds.) Grid Computing: Software Environments and Tools. Springer-Verlag, New York, USA, pp. 205-229.

Cao H, Jin H, Wu S, Qi L (2006) Serviceflow: Qos based service composition in cgsp. In: EDOC '06: Proceedings of the 10th IEEE International Enterprise Distributed Object Computing Conference. IEEE Computer Society, Washington, DC, USA, pp. 453-458.

Caromel D, di Costanzo A, Delbe C (2007) Peer-to-peer and fault-tolerance: Towards deployment-based technical services. Future Generation Computer Systems, 23(7):879-887.

Costen F, Brooke J, Pettipher M (1999) Investigation to make best use of lsf with high efficiency. In: IWCC '99: Proceedings of the 1st IEEE Computer Society International Workshop on Cluster Computing. IEEE Computer Society, Washington, DC, USA, p. 211.

Czajkowski K, Foster IT, Karonis NT, Kesselman C, Martin S, Smith W, Tuecke S (1998) A resource management architecture for metacomputing systems. In: IPPS/SPDP '98: Proceedings of the Workshop on Job Scheduling Strategies for Parallel Processing. Springer-Verlag, London, UK, pp. 62-82.

Erwin DW (2002) Unicore—a grid computing environment. Concurrency and Computation-Practice & Experience, 14(13-15): 1395-1410.

Fieseler T, Gürich W (2008) Operation of the core d-grid infrastructure. In: CCGRID '08: Proceedings of the 2008 8th IEEE International Symposium on Cluster Computing and the Grid. IEEE Computer Society, Washington, DC, USA, pp. 162-168.

Gong Y, Dong F, Li W, Xu Z (2003) Vega infrastructure for resource discovery in grids. J Comput Sci Technol, 18(4): 413-422.

Henderson RL (1995) Job scheduling under the portable batch system. In: IPPS '95: Proceedings of the Workshop on Job Scheduling Strategies for Parallel Processing, Springer-Verlag, London, UK, pp. 279-294.

Huang W, Wu Y, Yuan Y, Liu J, Yang G, Zheng W (2007) Parallel programming over Chinagrid. Int J Web Grid Serv, 3(4):480-497.

Jin H (2004) Chinagrid: Making grid computing a reality. In: Chen Z, Chen H,

Miao Q, Fu Y, Fox E, Lim E (eds.) Digital Libraries: International Collaboration and Cross-Fertilization. Springer, Singapore, pp. 13-24.

Kunszt P, Badino P, Frohner A, McCance G, Nienartowicz K, Rocha R, Rodrigues D (2005) Data storage, access and catalogs in glite. In: LGDI '05: Proceedings of the 2005 IEEE International Symposium on Mass Storage Systems and Technology. IEEE Computer Society, Washington, DC, USA, pp. 166-170.

Laszewski, Smith W, Tuecke S (1997) A directory service for configuring highperformance distributed computations. In: HPDC '97: Proceedings of the 6th IEEE International Symposium on High Performance Distributed Computing. IEEE Computer Society, Washington, DC, USA, p. 365.

Li L, Shi W, Lin J, Jiang L, Li L (2008) Cgsp-dai a heterogeneous databases access and integration on cgsp. In: ISCSCT '08: Proceedings of the 2008 International Symposium on Computer Science and Computational Technology. IEEE Computer Society, Washington, DC, USA, pp. 480-484.

Liu L, Wu Y, Yang G, Ma R, He F (2006) General running service: An execution framework for executing legacy program on grid. In: GCCW '06: Proceedings of the Fifth International Conference on Grid and Cooperative Computing Workshops. IEEE Computer Society, Washington, DC, USA, pp. 522-529.

Ma RY, Meng XX, Liu SJ, Wu YW (2006) Execution management in ChinaGrid supporting platform. In: GCC '06: Proceedings of the 15th International Conference on Grid and Cooperative Computing. IEEE Computer Society, Washington, DC, USA, pp. 249-256.

Ma RY, Wu YW, Meng XX, Liu SJ, Pan L (2008) Grid-enabled workflow management system based on bpel. Int J High Perform Comput Appl, 22(3):238-249.

Marco C, Fabio C, Alvise D, Antonia G, Francesco G, Alessandro M, Moreno M, Salvatore M, Fabrizio P, Luca P, Francesco P (2009) The glite workload management system. In: GPC '09: Proceedings of the 4th International Conference on Advances in Grid and Pervasive Computing. Springer-Verlag, Berlin, Heidelberg, pp. 256-268.

Munro C, Koblitz B, Santos N, Khan A (2006) Measurement of the lcg2 and glite file catalogue's performance. IEEE Transactions on Nuclear Science, 53(4): 2228-2232.

Qi L, Jin H, Foster I, Gawor J (2007) Hand: Highly available dynamic deployment infrastructure for globus toolkit 4. In: Vecchia GD, di Serafino D, Marra I, Perla F (eds.) 15th Euromicro International Conference on Parallel, Distributed and Network-Based Processing (PDP 2007). IEEE Computer Society, Naples, Italy, pp. 155-162.

Reed DA (2003) Grids, the teragrid and beyond. IEEE Computer, 36(1): 62-68.

Skovira J, Chan W, Zhou H, Lifka DA (1996) The easy—loadleveler api project. In: IPPS '96: Proceedings of the Workshop on Job Scheduling Strategies for Parallel Processing. Springer-Verlag, London, UK, pp. 41-47.

Wang C (2006) Dynamic access control prediction for ordered service sequence in grid environment. In: WI '06: Proceedings of the 2006 IEEE/WIC/ACM International Conference on Web Intelligence. IEEE Computer Society, Washington, DC, USA, pp. 145-151.

Wei XH, Li WW, Tatebe O, Xu GC, Hu L, Ju JB (2005) Integrating local job scheduler—lsf^{TM} with gfarm^{TM}. In: ISPA'05 International Conference on Parallel and Distributed Processing and Applications. Springer, Berlin, pp. 196-204.

Welch V (2004) Globus toolkit version 4 grid security infrastructure: A standards perspective. URL http://www-unix.globus.org/toolkit/docs/development/4.0-drafts/security/GT4-GSI-Overview.pdf.

Wu S, Jin H, Xiong M, Wang W (2007a) Data management services and transfer scheme in Chinagrid. Int J Web Grid Serv, 3(4): 447-461.

Wu S, Xiao K, Qi L (2007b) Gpe4cgsp: interoperability between heterogeneous grid infrastructures. In: China HPC '07: Proceedings of the 2007 Asian Technology Information Program's (ATIP's) 3rd Workshop on High performance computing in China. ACM, New York, NY, USA, pp. 110-114.

Wu Y, Liu L, Zheng W, He F (2006) On interoperability: The execution management perspective based on Chinagrid support platform. In: GCCW '06: Proceedings of the 5th International Conference on Grid and Cooperative Computing Workshops. IEEE Computer Society, Washington, DC, USA, pp. 86-93.

Wu Y, Yuan Y, Yang G, Zheng W (2007) Load prediction using hybrid model for computational grid. In: GRID '07: Proceedings of the 8th IEEE/ACM International Conference on Grid Computing. IEEE Computer Society, Washington, DC, USA, pp. 235-242.

Wu Y, Yuan Y, Yang G, Zheng W (2010) An adaptive task-level fault-tolerant approach to grid. J Supercomput, 51(2):97-114.

Zhang H, Zhou X, Yang Z, Wu X, Luo Y (2006) Grid information service architecture in Chinagrid. In: GCC '06: Proceedings of the 5th International Conference on Grid and Cooperative Computing. IEEE Computer Society, Washington, DC, USA, pp. 307-310.

3

Highly Available Dynamic Deployment Infrastructure

Abstract: To effectively support dynamic provisioning, an adaptive infrastructure which enables host-swapping and fault tolerance is necessary. Addressing this challenge, we propose a Highly Available Dynamic Deployment Infrastructure (HAND), based on the Java Web Services Core of Globus Toolkit 4. HAND provides capability, availability and extensibility for dynamic deployment of Java Web Services in dynamic grid environments. We identify the factors that can impact dynamic deployment in static and dynamic environments. We also present the design, analysis, implementation and evaluation of two different approaches to dynamic deployment (service level and container-level). We also examine the performance of an alternative data transfer protocol for service implementations. The results demonstrate that HAND can deliver significantly improved availability and performance relative to other approaches.

3.1 Motivation

As discussed in Chapter 2, a grid is an Internet-connected computing environment in which computing and data resources are geographically distributed in different administrative domains, often with separate policies for security and resource use. With the introduction of OGSA (Foster *et al.*, 2002), the focus of grid computing moved from legacy computing-intensive applications to service-oriented computing based on open standards. Globus Toolkit (GT) development has tracked this trend, with GT4 (Foster, 2006) building on the Web Service Resource Framework (WSRF) specifications to provide an efficient, extensible, stateful and flexible grid middleware.

Experience within ChinaGrid (Jin, 2004) and elsewhere (Erwin, 2002; Gagliardi and Begin, 2005; Hailong *et al.*, 2006) has emphasized the importance of dynamic service deployment and management as an enabler of dynamically extensible virtual organizations (VOs) (Foster *et al.*, 2001). More specifically, we identify the following requirements when services are hosted on a dynamic management-enabled grid:

• Services must adapt at runtime to changes of scale in VOs and to changes in the number of users.

• It must be easy to reconfigure, redeploy and undeploy services, without shutting down the whole system.

• Grid software provisioning must take into account dynamic and unpredictable service demand from VO members.

• The availability of target management units for service requests should be maximized.

• Dynamic features should result in minimal development and management costs; that is, users must not be required to implement numerous interfaces or rules for dynamic deployment features.

Dynamic deployment is a big challenge: Frequent shutting down and starting up of services for software upgrades or changes in resources or users can increase management costs. Some dynamic deployment solutions have been proposed based on Apache Tomcat's dynamic deployment functionality (Smith and Anderson, 2004; Smith *et al.*, 2004; Weissman *et al.*, 2005). However, that infrastructure provides poor performance and availability, with the consequence that (for example) dynamic deployment during a workflow's execution can cause a critical task to fail. In another scenario, if a deployment operation is delayed or canceled because the target container is unavailable, the dependent task would also be delayed or canceled.

Before discussing the design and implementation of our dynamic deployment infrastructure, we introduce some basic concepts:

• Containers in a Web services-based system, such as GT4, host, service and execute user requests issued by clients that invoke operations defined by those services.

• The term dynamic deployment denotes the ability for remote clients to request the upload and deployment of new services into, or the undeployment of existing services from, existing containers.

• Issues of correctness and performance are of particular importance when service requests and deployment requests occur concurrently.

We define availability in a dynamic deployment infrastructure as the proportion of time when a system is in a functioning condition. The meaning of "functioning" is different for two types of clients.

- End users of services deployed in the container care about the success rate of their requests and the response time of those requests. Key issues for these users are the extent to which a container becomes inaccessible during dynamic deployment, and any overhead imposed on ordinary requests by the dynamic service infrastructure (e.g. due to locking).

- Users who deploy services, typically administrators, care about both the success rate and average time cost of the dynamic deployment requests themselves.

Based on these considerations, we adopt as metrics, the success rate of user requests, the average time cost for deployment requests and the deployment availability.

To implement highly available and capable dynamic deployment functionality, we propose HAND. The design of HAND is intended to meet six criteria:

• A container that receives a dynamic deployment request should complete existing user requests if possible, while ensuring that the dynamic deployment request is accepted as scheduled.

• User requests received during execution of a dynamic deployment procedure should be handled correctly if possible.

• When a dynamic deployment procedure is finished, user requests for newly installed services should be handled correctly.

• The deployment procedure should be decomposed into smaller steps to reduce the risk of deadlock. Generally, deadlocks in the dynamic deployment procedure arise when threads use common runtime resources (e.g. the common ClassLoaders) concurrently. Simplifying and decomposing the deployment steps into smaller substeps can reduce the time that the deployment threads and ordinary threads occupy shared resources.

• Multiple redundancy approaches should be provided to both remote and local users in order to reduce unavailability. If one approach proves to be unavailable, a user or container can adopt other approaches as backup to finish the deployment.

• The performance of the deployment procedure should be optimized to decrease the possibility of conflict between ordinary and deployment requests. In short, the overhead caused by the dynamic deployment infrastructure should be as small as possible for the ordinary requests.

In the following, we explore how our performance metrics can be maximized and how these criteria meet via two different approaches to dynamic deployment:

• Service-level deployment (HAND-S), in which we deactivate one or more existing services, install new services and re-activate those services, without reloading the whole container.

• Container-level deployment (HAND-C), in which the installation of any new service involves reloading (reinitializing and reconfiguring) the whole container.

We shall describe implementation techniques for both approaches and present experimental results that demonstrate that when HAND works concurrently in a dynamic network environment, it can deliver capability and availability that are acceptable and that meet the criteria described above.

3.2   Principle of Dynamic Deployment Infrastructure

Provisioning is an important feature in cluster computing and has been included in the OGSA specification (Foster *et al.*, 2002). However, the GT3 and GT4 releases of the Globus Toolkit Java Web Service Core have not addressed dynamic service deployment.

Weissman *et al.* (2005) have implemented dynamic deployment in GT by building on the dynamic deployment-enabled Apache Tomcat server as the hosting environment. With this approach, users package their services with the basic Java WS Core libraries as a WAR file and deploy it into Tomcat as a Web application. With the help of Tomcat Manager, the user can redeploy this application dynamically without restarting Tomcat or interfering with other Web applications.

An alternative approach (adopted here) is to refactor the kernel structure of the Java WS Core standalone container. This approach is more complicated as it requires low-level changes to the container. However, we gain the benefit of a more lightweight dynamic deployment implementation and simpler management. With this approach, we can use the grid archive (GAR) format for services and reuse GT's existing deployment mechanism. The result, as we shall show, is a highly available dynamic deployment infrastructure.

Weighing these advantages and disadvantages, we designed and implemented HAND in three parts, as illustrated in Fig. 3.1. The shaded components, Service Package Manager, Auto Deployer and Local Directory Listener, are optional; they are provided to support future advanced provisioning features.

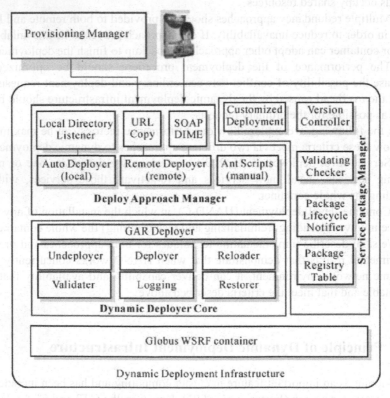

Fig. 3.1. Dynamic deployment modules

3.2.1   Dynamic Deployer Core

The Dynamic Deployer Core (DDC) is the kernel to realize the dynamic deployment in HAND and meet the criteria described in Section 3.1. The challenge in the DDC is to resolve two factors:

• The deactivation and activation of the services and container;

• The update of the runtime context in JVM, especially in the case of dynamic and multiple ClassLoaders.

To address time costs and safety issues, we use two ClassLoaders to isolate manageable services from system services. The common ClassLoader is responsible for the basic libraries used to run the container such as the XML parser, the SOAP engine, logging and security; this ClassLoader is not reloadable. The service ClassLoader is responsible for loading service libraries and is fully reloadable.

As shown in Fig. 3.1, DDC is comprised of seven parts. The GAR Deployer is in charge of invoking the actual deployment actions. In HAND, a reloading action can be safely executed once all services are shut down but before a new service ClassLoader is obtained. The Undeployer, Reloader and Deployer are reloading actions that can be passed from the Deploy Approach Manager to the GAR Deployer. Reloading action can update the service libraries, configuration files and so forth. The Validater is responsible for checking the correctness of the GAR file that is being deployed. It prevents DCC from deploying invalid or malformed GAR files. The Logging module is used to record a detailed log of the execution of the reloading actions. Finally, the Restorer is a simple backup mechanism. In case of an error it can help the container to restore its previous working state.

3.2.2   Deploy Approach Manager

The Deploy Approach Manager (DAM) is taken as inputing a GAR file in Java archive format. This file consists of a Web Service Deployment Descriptor (WSDD), WSRF resource descriptor files, application implementations and stubs. The GAR file might contain zero or more services.

DAM addresses our desire for redundant approaches (Criteria-5) by extending GT4 to provide three approaches to the service deployment.

The Auto Deployer is an experimental component that allows users to deploy and undeploy a target GAR file into a container by copying it into a specific directory on the local file system. This feature is convenient for local administrators.

The Ant Scripts are intended for the offline approach of deploying and undeploying the GARs. This approach works only when the container is off. This restriction is necessary in order to prevent conflicts that could arise when deploying into a running container.

The Remote Deployer is a standard WSRF service deployed in DDC. Named

DeployService, this service supports five operations: upload, download, deploy, undeploy and reload. The first two operations provide two different approaches to transferring a GAR file that is to be deployed to the container:

• Via SOAP with attachments using the upload() function. The GAR file is attached to the request.

• Via the download() function. The request specifies a URL (HTTP/S, GridFTP/FTP, etc.) for the GAR file, and the DeployService uses globus-url-copy to copy the GAR file from that URL location to the local file system.

Once a GAR file is transferred, the DeployService returns an identifier for the GAR. The GAR file can then be deployed by calling the deploy() function with that identifier. Once a GAR file is deployed, the DeployService deletes the file automatically.

A deployed service can be undeployed via the undeploy() operation. In addition, a client can reload the entire container by invoking the reload() operation, which restarts the container without executing any deployment actions. This operation is useful when a service or container configuration has been changed.

The DeployService publishes two resource properties:

• *Undeployable*: A list of GAR identifiers that can be undeployed.

• *Deployable*: A list of GAR identifiers that have been transferred to the service but not yet deployed.

GSI authentication and authorization are used to ensure that only authorized clients can invoke the DeployService operations.

3.2.3   Service Package Manager

The optional Service Package Manager (SPM) provides higher-level management features. In particular, the Package Lifecycle and Package Registry Table maintain information necessary for the service-level implementation. Since each GAR file may contain several services, service-level management can't be based on a simple GAR file management system. In our service-level implementation, SPM communicates with DDC to manage the target services dynamically. The SPM also includes three components, Version Controller, Customized Deployment and Validating Checker, which complete the complicated service-level grid software version control and online upgrades in different VOs.

• *Version Controller* is responsible for the version management of different services. It also provides metadata about cross-dependencies for the container system. It avoids upgrades of different applications' JARs.

• *Customized Deployment* permits remote users to submit their own deployment scripts; for example, a user can deploy an RPM package to a target system.

• *Validating Checker* is similar to the DDC Validater. A minor difference is that it focuses on more complicated dependencies and conflict checking among different services before deployment.

3.3   Service-Level vs. Container-Level

We define two approaches in the effort to meet Criteria-5 for dynamic deployment:
• In container-level deployment (HAND-C) the entire container is reloaded; all services in the container are deactivated and reactivated.
• In service-level deployment (HAND-S) a single service that is being deployed or undeployed is deactivated and reactivated. All other services are unaffected.

We have implemented both approaches within GT4. The container-level implementation is complete and has been merged into the GT code repository. The service-level implementation is a prototype, suitable for performance studies but not yet for production use.

Both approaches are important and useful in different scenarios, as we now discuss. Container-level deployment works well when a global upgrade or configuration is needed, while service-level deployment is more flexible and available in dynamic environments.

3.3.1   HAND-C: Container-Level Deployment

Container-level deployment proceeds as follows to reload a service implementation:
• Put the container in "reloading mode". The container will then return "service unavailable" error to any request that the container receives during the deployment. This step is blocked until all currently executing requests finish or until a specified timeout expires (whichever occurs first).
• Stop and deactivate all services, resource homes, and so forth.
• Perform cleanup operations to flush caches that might contain references to the resources and classes loaded by the original deployment.
• Execute the deployment or undeployment scripts.
• Reload the whole container. Configuration descriptor files, etc. are re-read and all services, resource homes, etc. are reactivated.
• Return the container to the normal operating mode and start accepting new requests.

This algorithm, in particular the use of timeouts in Step 1, seeks to balance the demands of Criteria-1 above with container stability. Steps 2 and 3 are executed to address Criteria-3. We note that this algorithm does not address Criteria-2. All user requests to a container are refused during any dynamic deployment operation on that container.

The timeline in Fig. 3.2 depicts a typical deployment operation. In this figure, "Service Session" denotes an execution of an ordinary request and "Deploy Session" denotes the execution of a deployment request. Moving from the top down, we first see a request that is interrupted due to the Step 1 timeout; then three requests that are completed successfully against the old service version; then the deployment request; then three requests that are refused because deployment is in progress; and finally two requests that are executed successfully against the new version of the service.

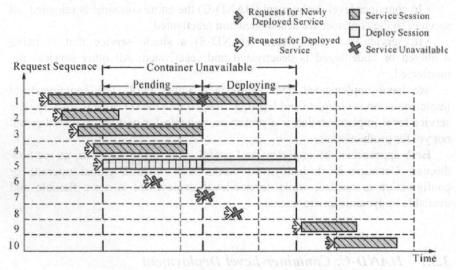

Fig. 3.2.   Container-level deployment available sequence

This approach is similar to that used in the Tomcat container. It has the following advantages:

• It avoids deadlock for it does not care about the dependencies among the services deployed in the container. It just reloads the whole container.

• It works well when we need to reload the whole service container, including the global configuration, service handlers and providers. In the case of an issued global installation and configuration or failed service-level reload operation, the container-level reload is significant in promising to keep the container stable.

• It minimizes memory and time costs in management, since all services share the same runtime context, i.e., the common service ClassLoader, unified deactivating or activating procedures and GAR management.

On the other hand, container-level deployment has disadvantages:

• (Re)deployment of any service results in the loss of the nonpersistent state associated with all services. While arguably no service implementation should make any assumptions concerning the availability of the nonpersistent state, in practice people often write services with such assumptions in mind. Thus, dynamic deployment can result in unpredictable behavior for clients.

• Deployment time is unpredictable when several parallel threads are involved (see Section 3.4.3).

3.3.2   HAND-S: Service-Level Deployment

Service-level deployment requires complete service isolation (including the service JAR files), a hierarchical ClassLoader tree (a separate ClassLoader for a set of services associated with a GAR file) and an SPM to manage the separate services. This approach allows us to address Criteria-2 of Section 1: The reduction in reloading granularity means that the deployment procedure need not impact requests to other services unrelated to those that are being deployed. Our service-level deployment logic meets these requirements as follows:

• Check the requested target service name. If it matches the DeployingService, then switch the ClassLoader to system level or use the normal services' own ClassLoader registered in the SPM. If requests are being processed that involve the services that are to be deployed, then suspend deployment until those requests are completed or a timeout occurs.

• Stop the services that are to be deployed if they are already running. During this period, the container will return "service unavailable" to any request to the services in the GAR file.

• Stop any services on which the pre-deployed services depend, and deactivate any related resources. Typically, these services are named in the pre-deployed GAR file.

• Perform cleanup operations to flush caches that might contain references to the classes loaded by the original deployment (just for redeploy).

• Execute the deployment or undeployment scripts.

• Create or update the working space context for the new services and then register to the SPM registry.

• Initialize, activate and start the new services.

The main difference between this approach and the container-level approach is that the reloading unit here is the service rather than the container as in HAND-C. Fig. 3.3 shows what happens when requests arrive during dynamic deployment in HAND-S. Requests 1, 2, 3, 4, 6 and 8 are to services other than the services being deployed, and can thus proceed without interruption. Only the 7th and 10th requests are to a service that is being deployed, and thus these two requests fail and succeed, respectively, as they occur during and after deployment.

Service-level deployment has the following advantages relative to the container-level deployment:

• The time required to reload a service is more predictable as it depends primarily on characteristics of that service, not other components deployed in the same container.

• Because there is no need to wait for and deactivate all services in the container, service-level deployment is much faster in most cases.

Service-level deployment also has limitations:

• There is a need for additional internal synchronization in the container, which can be costly. The container should switch among different ClassLoaders to match the various service requests, and must also maintain consistency with persistent storage (an XML file in our implementation), JNDI resources and Caches existing in service instances. Furthermore, HAND-S can't handle circular dependencies among services well (The dependency of service composition is another critical challenge in a grid which will be discussed in the next chapter).

• The need for a more detailed registry results in increased memory usage and execution time costs.

• If the registry structure is destroyed or the global configuration is updated, we must use container-level deployment to reinitialize the whole container.

• HAND-S will cost additional time and memory to check the service dependencies (see Section 3.3.3).

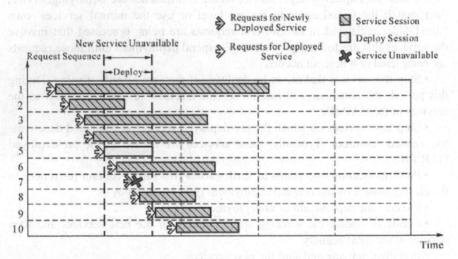

Fig. 3.3. Service-level deployment available sequence

3.3.3 Service Dependency

HAND-C avoids the service dependencies because it just executes the "stop" and "start" to reload the whole container. However, HAND-S has to issue it because the versioning problem of newly deployed services may crash the container.

Fig. 3.4 depicts a typical tree structure of ClassLoaders in HAND-S. Services A, B, C are packed in three deployed GARs respectively. As shown in the figure, A depends on B and C, while C depends on B. The term "depends on" means that source service requires the ClassLoaders of destination services to load dependent classes. Obviously, reloading GAR_2 (including B) will drive C and A to be unpredictable; meanwhile, reloading GAR_n (including C) will crash the execution of A. How to promise safety in redeploying the dependent services in HAND-S is a big challenge. We provide two optional policies to resolve the conflict.

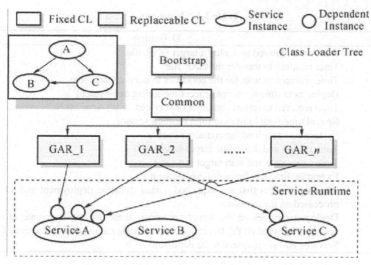

Fig. 3.4. Service-level deployment available sequence

3.3.4 Avoid Deadlock

Based on the experience from Havender (1968), the deadlock is caused by the competition for common resources. In HAND, the multiple threads mechanism provided by GT Web Service Java Core issues this. The thread for processing deployment requests is the producer, while the threads for executing ordinary requests are consumers. All of the non-destroyed resources lead to the deadlock. We take a series of solutions to avoid the deadlock in HAND-S.

• Producer thread is unique in the container all the time.

• Producer gets the resources collectively after the consumers are finished or interrupted. To put it simply, they are in a fixed order.

• The allocated resources could be released by force when a timeout occurs.

• Criteria-4 is efficient to avoid deadlock.

HAND-S provides a simple strategy to detect possible deadlock when circular service dependency is issued: SPM will put the related services in a stack recursively. Once a repeated one is found, HAND-S will execute Force Policy to restart all circular services forcedly.

3.3.5 Time Cost Analysis

We now discuss the costs associated with the two deployment approaches. We use the symbols in Table 3.1.

Table 3.1   Notations

Notation	Definition
t_{total}	Total time required to deploy a target GAR file
$t_{transfer}$	Time required to transfer the GAR file
$t_{pending}$	Time required to wait for the container to become available
t_{deploy}	Deployment time for script processing during deployment
t_{reload}	Time required to restart container or services
t_{limit}	Reload timed-out limitation for a running service
t_{system}	System cost to reload the container itself
t_i	Time to stop and deactivate target service i
t_i'	Time to activate and start target service i
s_i	Execution time left for unfinished request i
R	Running services that are requested during dynamic deployment and are being processed on the container
D	Deployed services on the target container; these are the aggregate of all the services deployed on the target container, whether activated or deactivated
D'	Services that are prepared to be deployed

To meet Criteria-4, as shown in Fig. 3.5, the deployment procedure in HAND consists of several phases: deployment preparation, physical deploying and reloading phase. The dashed "Pending" box indicates that it depends on the concrete approach (HAND-S or HAND-C) chosen to issue the reloading.

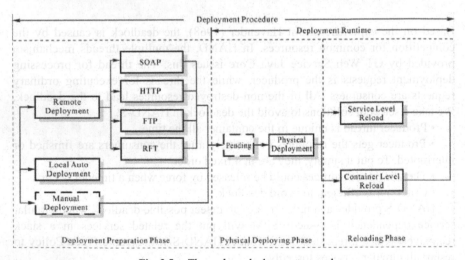

Fig. 3.5.   Three-phase deployment procedure

The total dynamic deployment time consists of four parts:

$$t_{total} = t_{transfer} + t_{pending} + t_{deploy} + t_{reloading} \qquad (3.1)$$

The t_{deploy} and $t_{transfer}$ components are determined by the deployment methods used in the preparation phase and the complexity of the ANT scripts that implement deployment actions, both of which are independent of the deployment procedure.

For HAND-C, t_{pending} and $t_{\text{reloading}}$ are as follows:

$$t_{\text{pending}} = \min\left(\max_R (s_i),\ t_{\text{limit}} \times \|R\|\right) \qquad (3.2)$$

$$t_{\text{reloading}} = \sum_{i=1}^{n}(t_i + t_i') + t_{\text{system}},\quad n = \|D\| \qquad (3.3)$$

Based on the discussion in Section 3.2, we conclude that the pending time is mainly spent waiting for completion of existing requests. Hence, the total time is the minimum of the maximum remaining time of the currently executing requests and the time required to interrupt for all running threads. The reloading time is equal to the system reloading time plus the deactivation and activation time for all deployed services.

For HAND-S, the pending time is the time spent waiting for completion of existing requests for the target service and any related services. Since the problem of service dependency is complicated, we will investigate it and discuss it in the following chapter. Here, we assume that related services D' are just the services defined in the GAR's Web Service Deployment Descriptor (WSDD) file. The reloading time shrinks to the sum of the deactivating time and activating time of the related services.

$$t_{\text{pending}} = \min(\max_{D' \cap R}(s_i), t_{\text{limit}} \times \|D' \cap R\|) \qquad (3.4)$$

$$t_{\text{reloading}} = \sum_{i \in D' \cap R} t_i + \sum_{i \in D'} t_i' \qquad (3.5)$$

We define t_{total} (HAND-S) and t_{total} (HAND-C) as the time cost for two approaches, and we assume that both approaches use the same deploying method and the same GAR file. The relationship between running services, predeployed services and deployed services is

$$D' \cap R \subseteq R \subseteq D \qquad (3.6)$$

If the processing requests are finished at the same time, then t_{pending} (*service*) $\leq$ t_{pending} (*container*). Similarly, we can achieve $t_{\text{reloading}}$ (*service*) $\leq$ $t_{\text{reloading}}$ (*container*). Hence, it is not too difficult to conclude that t_{total} (*service*) $\leq$ t_{total} (*container*) in a dynamic invocation environment.

3.4   Performance Analysis

A comprehensive evaluation of dynamic deployment is challenging because of the difficulty of capturing the complexities of a realistic grid environment. Thus, we focus on micro-benchmarks designed to capture specific aspects of dynamic deployment behavior, namely, deployment time, capability, availability and file transfer performance.

3.4.1   Dynamic Deployment Experiments

As discussed in Section 3.3, the service container becomes unavailable during dynamic deployment. Thus, we first measured deployment time as a function of both the size of the file being deployed and the number of services in the container.

The experimental setup was as follows. We installed and tested the HAND containers at two sites: a local site with three PC servers, powered by Pentium VI 2.4 GHz with 2 GB RAM and 37 GB hard disk in a cluster; and a remote site equipped with one PC server, powered by Pentium III 1 GHz with 1,024 MB RAM. The two sites were connected by a 2.5 GB fabric WAN shared with other CERNET applications. The local cluster was connected with 100 MB Ethernet. All tests ran on Fedora 3 with Linux kernel 2.6.9 – 1.667. The Java version was Java 2 Software Development Kit (J2SDK) 1.4.2_08-b03 and we used -Xms64m and -Xmx1024m parameters to enlarge the maximum JVM memory.

We constructed a set of grid archive (GAR) files for use in our experiments, as summarized in Table 3.2. The first 5 files ranged in size from 42 KB to 100 MB, a range typically encountered in grid applications. We also constructed a large number of identical services, testService_clone0 to testService_cloneN, for evaluating the impact of the number of deployed services on performance. The Jars column in Table 3.2 denotes how many JAR files were in the package; the Compress Ratio column is the ratio of the compressed file size to the original.

Table 3.2   Test packages used in the experiments

ID	Package	Size(KB)	Jars	Compress Ratio
1	testService1.gar	42	2	63%
2	testService2.gar	1,154	4	33%
3	testService3.gar	12,909	56	90%
4	testService4.gar	42,236	61	75%
5	testService5.gar	98,004	59	55%
6...*n*	testService_cloneN.gar	40	2	63%

We measured the time required to deploy each of the files 1 – 5 of Table 3.2 into a container running 9 services, the basic service set deployed by default by GT. The only request made during the dynamic deployment procedure was that to

DeployService. Each deployment was repeated 40 times. We present the deployment and reloading times (as discussed in Section 3.3); the pending time is zero in this case.

Fig. 3.6 gives our results. Timers in our implementation allow us to break down the total deployment time into the following categories:
• Deploy (D), which includes the physical deployment time (D-D) and reloading time (D-R) as discussed in Section 3.3.
• Redeploy (R), which includes the physical redeployment time (R-D) and reloading time (R-R).
• Undeploy (U), which also includes the physical undeployment time (U-D) and reloading time (U-R).

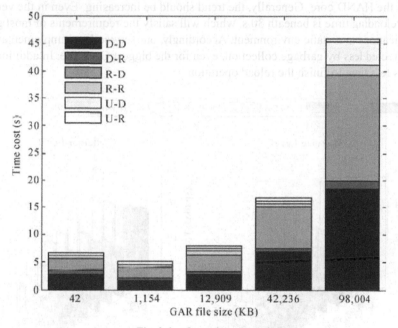

Fig. 3.6. Operation comparisons

The time required to execute physical deployment scripts is the biggest cost in the Deploy operation (D); the physical redeployment time (R-D) cost is slightly greater than that. Each redeploy operation consists of a sequence of undeploy and deploy operations. In HAND-C, the first step of deployment is to check whether or not the new GAR is already deployed. Undeploy simply deletes all deployed files and reloads the container; the time cost is decided mainly by U-D, which naturally increases with GAR file size. Thus, we can determine that the reloading time, equal to the difference between the operation times (D/R/U) and the physical deployment times (D-D/R-D/U-D), increases slowly as the GAR size changes. Initially, the biggest time cost of an atomic operation is just less than 20 s, which we believe is tolerable for most grid applications.

To identify additional impact factors on deployment and reloading costs, we enlarged the deployed service scale from 9 to 879 services. Fig. 3.7 shows the results of this new experiment. In this figure, the z axis expresses the time cost for reloading the container. The results show that reloading time increases with the number of services. In the service scale, the reloading time of different-sized GAR files is nearly the same when the GAR file size is less than 42 MB. However, the time increases rapidly when the GAR file size increases to about 100 MB. The results show nearly the same linearity in smaller GAR files (42 KB to 42 MB), but become bumpy when the GAR file size increases to about 100 MB. The reason is that the JVM's garbage collector runs in the background randomly. When the deployed service size is big enough, garbage collection shares the reloading time with the HAND core. Generally, the trend should be increasing. Even in the vertex, the reloading time is beneath 30 s, which will satisfy the requirements of most grid applications in a static environment. Accordingly, our service-level implementation is affected less by garbage collection, even for the biggest GAR file. In addition, it costs less time to finish the reload operation.

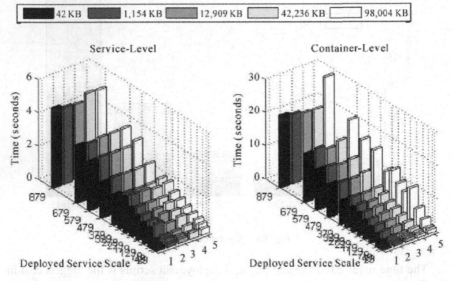

Fig. 3.7.   Scaled comparison on reload

Based on the results from Fig. 3.7, we discard the bumpy container-level data and then attempt to fit a curve to our two sets of data. We define x as the deployed service scale and y as the reloading time cost, and assume k-th degree polynomial as:

$$y = a_0 + a_1 x + \cdots + a_k x^k \tag{3.7}$$

The residual is given by

$$R^2 = \sum_{i=0}^{n} [y_i - (a_0 + a_1 x_i + \cdots + a_k x_i^k)]^2 \tag{3.8}$$

By using least quadratic fitting technique, we filled in our data and finally found that, when k equals 2, we could get the fittest polynomial for two levels. As the formulas list below, y_c is the container-level time cost polynomial and y_s is the service-level.

$$y_c = 0.0106x^2 + 13.478x + 372.5, \ R^2 = 0.997 \tag{3.9}$$

$$y_s = 0.0018x^2 + 3.5468x + 235.86, \ R^2 = 0.991 \tag{3.10}$$

Fig. 3.8 denotes our fit curves. We see that service-level reloads are less expensive than container-level reloads in all circumstances. This result confirms our earlier analyses and matches our conclusions in previous sections. We note that the availability of sufficient memory for service-level deployment is an important precondition for this result.

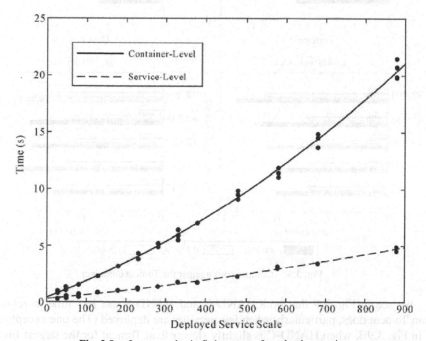

Fig. 3.8. Least quadratic fitting curve for reload operation

From Eqs. (3.9) and (3.10), we see that if no services are deployed, both approaches incur a reload cost of around 300 ms. And in both cases, the polynomial times are all $O(x^2)$.

To enable direct comparison with other dynamic deployment enabled containers, we repeated our experiments on the Apache Tomcat container (version 5.0.30), as used by Weissman *et al.* (2005) (However, note that we use GT4, not GT3 as used by those authors). Also, we increased the JVM memory to 1 GB by adding the '-Xms64m -Xmx1024m' parameter. Fig. 3.9 presents the experimental results in the different service-level (10, 200, 400 and 600 services) environment. In this figure, HAND-C is our container-level implementation. HAND-S is the service-level implementation and TOMCAT denotes the Apache Tomcat hosting environment.

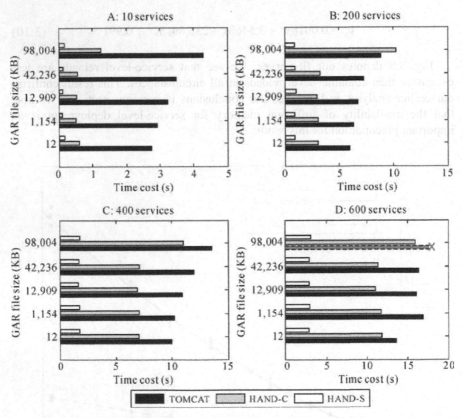

Fig. 3.9.   Comparisons against the Tomcat container

We see in Fig. 3.9 that both HAND-C and HAND-S use less time to reload than Tomcat does, particularly when few services are deployed (The one exception is in Fig. 3.9B, when HAND-C is slightly slower than Tomcat for the largest file). This effect is particularly evident in the case of our service-level implementation (Tomcat is a container-level implementation), but is also evident in the case of the container-level implementation, presumably because Tomcat typically deactivates or activates more components, including Apache Axis itself, cluster components, Jasper and the like. The HAND core, however, mainly involves only Apache Axis and just reloads the ClassLoader and updates the JNDI tree appropriately. In Fig. 3.9D, Tomcat issues an "out of memory" exception for the largest GAR file, which particularly concerns our desire for container stability.

As shown above, if support for massive dynamic deployment-enabled applications is needed, one should use the HAND container instead of Tomcat to guarantee capability, usability and reliability.

3.4.2 *Capability and Availability in Dynamic Environment*

Our next experiments were designed to study interactions between service deployment operations and other requests to a container. We designed these experiments as follows:

• We first dynamically deployed 8 cloned services that take, respectively, 0, 30, 60, 90, 120, 180, 240 and 330 s to process a user request.

• We then started 4 client threads, each of which issued a series of 1,000 invocations, and each to one of the 8 services started in Step 1. These threads also logged both failed and successful invocations.

• We also started a thread that issued a series of 100 deploy requests at random intervals during the period of Step 2. Each such request deployed, redeployed and undeployed one of a second set of 10 cloned services.

We ran experiments on both HAND-C and HAND-S, and used 4 parallel threads to do our experiments, which is the high water mark of the GT4 Java core container (i.e., the medium overhead of the GT container). We configured the GT4 container with 35 deployed services, which means (based on the results of Section 3.4.1) that HAND-C should incur a reloading cost of 875 ms and HAND-S a cost of 362 ms. Finally, we note that all deployed services are unrelated in logic: i.e., services in different GARs do not invoke the others' ClassLoaders.

Fig. 3.10 shows that the deployment time increases rapidly with service serving time for HAND-C, due to the need to wait for the completion of service invocations that are already in progress. When service serving time is long enough (the cross mark in the figure), namely greater than the reloading timed-out limitation (default 5 minutes in HAND-C), the deployment operation is canceled, due to the client timeout of 10 minutes. In contrast, while HAND-S deployment time is initially slightly higher than that for HAND-C, it then stays fairly constant as service serving time increases.

Fig. 3.11 shows that HAND-S also achieves consistently high success rates. This result is as expected, given that the reload of one service does not affect other services in the same container. In contrast, the HAND-C success rate is low and unpredictable. When the service serving time grows above the reload timed-out limitation, most client invocations are canceled because of client timeout.

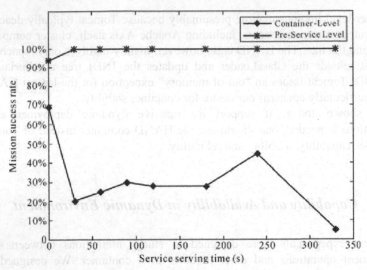

Fig. 3.10. Deployment time in a dynamic environment

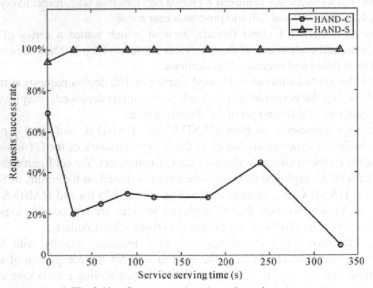

Fig. 3.11. Success rate in a dynamic environment

In Table 3.3, we show the average deployment time for both HAND-S and HAND-C across these experiments. Our results indicate that the capability of dynamic deployment at the container-level is unpredictable in a complicated dynamic grid environment. The cost stems from promising the success rate of the requests before dynamic deployment and preventing deadlock during container restart. Moreover, the success rate of normal service requests also decreases when deployment is triggered. This level is suitable for clients that incorporate some fault tolerance logic.

Table 3.3 Comparison of deployment time and success rate

	HAND-S	HAND-C
Average deployment time (ms)	6,849.57	85,487.94
Average success rate (%)	99.25	31.13

We conclude that service-level deployment is more capable and more available than container-level deployment for dynamic and complicated grid environments.

3.4.3 GAR File Transfer Performance

Our third set of experiments focused on the performance of the DAM file transfer function. We evaluate the performance of three transfer protocols in LAN and WAN environments. The test packages used the five GAR files, which were invoked 20 times each.

Figs. 3.12 and 3.13 show that in both LAN and WAN, the SOAP attachment in DIME format approach costs more than HTTP or FTP. When the GAR file size is near to, or less than, 10 MB, the SOAP attachment is convenient for users to transfer the target files directly from the client. For larger files, it is advisable to choose GridFTP, FTP or HTTP. Especially in a WAN environment, transferring big GAR files by SOAP attachment will cost more time and more server memory, and may even cause the server to run out of memory. Compared with HTTP, FTP may provide better access control and flow control. For secure and reliable transfers, the GT4 GridFTP (Allcock *et al.*, 2004) and Reliable File Transfer (RFT) service (Allcock *et al.*, 2005) are recommended, although we note that's because GridFTP use of public key authentication to impose a startup overhead relative to traditional FTP.

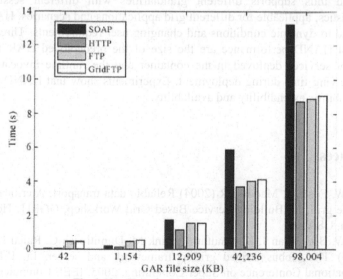

Fig. 3.12. Transferring efficiency in LAN

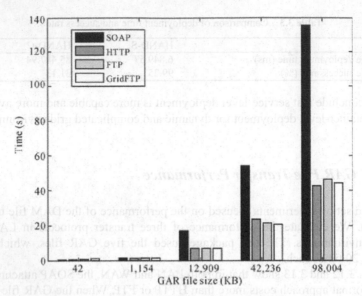

Fig. 3.13.   Transferring efficiency in WAN

3.5   Summary

In this chapter we have described HAND, a highly available dynamic deployment infrastructure for use in the Globus Toolkit Java Web Services container. HAND addresses dynamic service deployment at both the container-level and the service level, and thus supports different granularities with different session lock characteristics, applicable for different grid applications and scenarios. HAND can be adapted to dynamic conditions and changing user requirements. Three factors that affect HAND performance are the size of the predeployed GAR files, the number of services deployed in the container and the runtime invocations and service serving time during deployment. Experiments show that HAND provides good capability, extendibility and availability.

References

Allcock W, Foster I, Madduri R (2004) Reliable data transport: A critical service for the grid. In: Building Service Based Grid Workshop, GGF11. Honolulu's Haiaii, USA.

Allcock W, Bresnahan J, Kettimuthu R, Link M, Dumitrescu C, Raicu I, Foster I (2005) The globus striped gridftp framework and server. In: IEEE/ACM International Conference on Super Computing, 2005. IEEE Computer Society,

Cambridge, Massachusetts, USA, pp. 54-62.

Erwin DW (2002) Unicore—a grid computing environment. Concurrency and Computation-Practice & Experience, 14(13-15): 1395-1410.

Foster I (2006) Globus toolkit version 4: software for service-oriented systems. Journal of Computer Science and Technology, 21(4): 513-520.

Foster I, Kesselman C, Tuecke S (2001) The anatomy of the grid: Enabling scalable virtual organizations. International Journal of High Performance Computing Applications, 15(3): 200-222.

Foster I, Kesselman C, Nick J, Tuecke S (2002) The physiology of the grid: An open grid services architecture for distributed systems integration. URL citeseer. ist.psu.edu/foster02physiology.html.

Gagliardi F, Begin ME (2005) Egee—providing a production quality grid for eScience. In: Local to Global Data Interoperability—Challenges and Technologies, 2005. IEEE Computer Society, Sardinia, Italy, pp. 88-92.

Sun H, Liu W, Wo T, Hu C (2006) Crown node server: An enhanced grid service container based on gt4 wsrf core. In: 5th International Conference on Grid and Cooperative Computing Workshops, 2006. IEEE Computer Society, Changsha, China, pp. 510-517.

Havender J (1968) Avoiding deadlock in multitasking systems. IBM Systems Journal, 7(2): 74-84.

Jin H (2004) ChinaGrid: Making grid computing a reality. In: Chen Z, Chen H, Miao Q, Fu Y, Fox E, Lim E (eds.) Digital Libraries: International Collaboration and Cross-Fertilization. Springer, Singapore, pp. 13-24.

Smith E, Anderson P (2004) Dynamic reconfiguration for grid fabrics. In: Buyya R (ed.) 5th IEEE/ACM International Workshop on Grid Computing, IEEE Computer Society, Pittsburgh, USA, pp. 86-93.

Smith M, Friese T, Freisleben B (2004) Towards a service-oriented ad hoc grid. In: 3rd International Workshop on Parallel and Distributed Computing, 2004. 3rd International Symposium on/Algorithms, Models and Tools for Parallel Computing on Heterogeneous Networks, 2004. IEEE Computer Society, Cork, Ireland, pp. 201-208.

Weissman JB, Kim S, England D (2005) A framework for dynamic service adaptation in the grid: Next generation software program progress report. In: 19th IEEE International Parallel and Distributed Processing Symposium, 2005. IEEE Computer Society, Denver, CA, USA, p. 5.

4

Service-Oriented Dependency-Aware Maintenance

Abstract: When the scale of a computational system grows from a single machine to a grid with thousands of nodes, the interdependencies among these resources and software components also become complicated. The maintenance of the increasingly distributed systems will face many challenges. One of the most important challenges is how to balance the efficiency of maintenance and the availability of a global system without shutting down the whole system. In this chapter, a novel mechanism, called Cobweb Guardian, is proposed to provide several solutions to avoid or reduce the effects of different dependencies, i.e., deployment dependency, invocation dependency and environment dependency. By using the Cobweb Guardian, administrators of a grid can execute the maintaining task safely in the runtime with high availability. The evaluation results show that our proposed dependency-aware maintenance can bring higher throughput and availability for a grid during maintenance in the runtime.

4.1 Dependency-Aware Maintenance

Today's Web or grid services are usually composed of several standalone services that encapsulate and present useful functionalities. Examples include (i) an online digital album which is composed of simple storage services and metadata management services; (ii) an execution management system that consists of information service, authentication and authorization services, data transferring service and so on. Within these composite services, the service components are partitioned, replicated and aggregated to achieve high availability and incremental scalability, especially when the system experiences high growth in service evolution and user demands. However, from the experience of ChinaGrid Support Platform (CGSP) (Wu *et al.*, 2005), the scale and complexity of Virtual Organizations (VO) (Foster *et al.*, 2001) make them increasingly difficult and expensive to manage and deploy. A system update at even a moderate scale data center in a VO might require changes to more than 1,000 machines, most of which might have interdependencies among themselves (Talwar *et al.*, 2005). That means any maintenance to a service component must be propagated or carefully contained so that the services using it continue to function correctly. Furthermore, the availability of global management units for service requests during maintenance require to be maximized too. During maintenance, the related services might have to be shut down temporally in traditional distributed systems. However, some critical upper business such as bank services must provide services continuously over 24 h. Any unpredictable pause in the maintenance will lead to a big loss.

Specifically, for the administrators of a specific grid, the maintenance for services is running through the whole lifecycle of service components. Each service component in grid has the lifecycle of: *released, deployed, initialed, activated and destroyed*. Responding to these stages, the maintaining tasks include publishing, deploying, undeploying, upgrading, configuring, activating and deactivating. How to coordinate these maintenances without scarifying the utilization of target resources and availability of the global system is indeed a great challenge.

As shown in Fig. 4.1, we take the realistic accounting logs from CGCL (a domain of ChinaGrid) as the example. During the observed 60 h (from 00:00:00 GMT+8 Jul. 18, 2008 to 12:00:00 GMT+8 Jul. 20, 2008), the grid infrastructure with 41 HPC nodes 3^1 was continuously serving the requests from ten users (Fig. 4.1(c)). Obviously, if the grid administrator has a plan to commit the upgrade of infrastructure services (e.g. transferring services, authentication services and so forth), it would be impossible to complete because there is no time slot to permit him to do that. In addition, all of the user applications were running upon those critical services. Even taking a sub-optimal solution, we ran the upgrades in a time slot (the 7th in Fig. 4.1(a)) during which there were the fewest running requests. Eventually, there would be 33 running services and 28 new requests failed (Fig. 4.1(b)). Furthermore, if the upgrade work can't be finished in an hour, more service requests will be rejected.

From this scenario, a more sophisticated maintaining mechanism would have benefited the administrator in many ways. First, the administrator need not do maintaining operations for each service component in serial each time. Next, the maintaining tool should evaluate the runtime invocation dependencies to decide which solution could provide higher availability. Moreover, multiple maintaining granularity should be supported in a maintaining mechanism to reduce the effects of the environment. Finally, the deployment (or versioning) dependencies between services could have been detected before the maintenance in advance, reducing the need to make changes and the likelihood of making errors in a specific maintenance.

Technology dependencies have been investigated throughout the desktop computing age (Sangal *et al.*, 2005; Yau and Tsai, 1987). They are widely used for optimizing an area of software engineering. However, the static and simple

---

[1] The detail configuration can be found at http://grid.hust.edu.cn/hpce/index.php

approaches can't guarantee efficiency and availability in the runtime for the components distributed widely in grids. This chapter recognizes the importance of distributed service maintenance and its challenges. The main goal of this study is to answer the following question. How to promise higher availability for a global system when a maintenance operation happens to a service component with complicated dependencies?

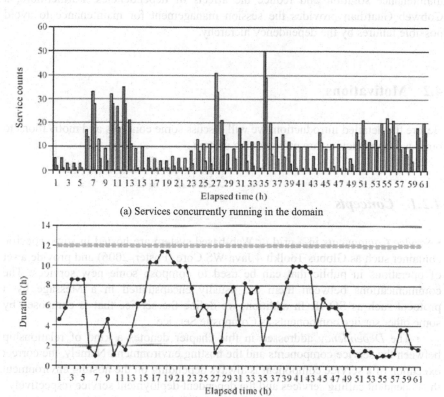

(a) Services concurrently running in the domain

(b) Services executing duration in the domain

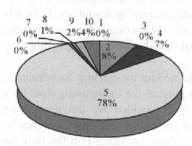

ID	User	Total(s)
1	bhhuang	1,402
2	dhpet	112,212
3	huangjiao	2,346
4	hzhang	103,245
5	klyao	1,084,012
6	kxiao	3,427
7	lb	4,282
8	test	7,210
9	vast	28,468
10	zhshao	52,195

(c) Top 10 users

Fig. 4.1.   Service running statistics in a domain of ChinaGrid

We propose a new mechanism, named Cobweb Guardian, which supports multiple granularities (service, container and node-level) maintenance for service components to reduce the affects from environment dependency. In addition, the Cobweb Guardian manages a different service dependencies map that is initially provided by automatic detector or grid administrators. When a maintenance request arrives, it recognizes the related dependency to generate an optimized maintenance solution and reduce the affects of dependencies. Furthermore, a Cobweb Guardian provides the session management for maintenance to avoid possible failures by the dependency hierarchy.

4.2   Motivations

Before the detailed introduction, we will discuss some concepts and motivations to build a dependency-aware provisioning system.

4.2.1   Concepts

• *Service Components* in a grid or Web-based system are hosted in some specific container such as Globus Toolkit 4 Java WS Core (Foster, 2006) and provide a set of operations in public that can be used to compose some new services. The communications between them are usually encapsulated in a Message by a protocol such as SOAP. In addition, we define the service that is composed by some other service components as Composite Service.

• The *Dependency* addressed in this chapter denotes a kind of relationship between the service components and the hosting environment. Namely, the correct execution of a service component is always depending on the hosting environment, the dependent calling services and the dependent deployment service respectively.

• The *Maintenance* of a grid or distributed Web services based system denotes a set of operations (e.g. deploy, undeploy and so on) to some particular service components distributed in the Internet-connected computing resources. Normally these requests are delivered by the administrators. By invoking the maintenances automatically, the grid system is capable of self-healing, self-growing and dynamical provisioning.

To state the problem clearly, two metrics are defined for the dynamic maintenance.

- Maintaining Time. In the distributed environment, the maintaining time for a specific service component (r) (marked as t) is decided by the time spent transferring maintenance related packages (e.g. installing packages, patches or configuration files (t_t), the time spent deploying these packages (t_d), the time for reloading essential components or container (t_r), and the time for pending invocation requests (t_p) due to dependencies. The pending and reloading periods are rather dynamical during the maintenance. Meanwhile, most components would be unavailable during the two periods. Eq. (4.1) denotes this equation.

$$t(r) = t_t + t_d + \sum_{s}^{S_r} [t_p(s) + t_r(s)] + t_r(r) \tag{4.1}$$

In Eq. (4.1), the S_r are the service components on which the service component r is depending. The $\sum_{s}^{S_r} [t_p(s) + t_r(s)]$ denotes that the pending time of r is decided by the related components recursively.

We suppose that the task covers n service components distributed in m resources. Ideally, the shortest maintaining time (lower bound) is for deploying n services to the resources in parallel. Vice versa, the most cost effective maintenance (upper bound) is to maintain the service components in different resources in series and with a possible penalty time. The actual maintaining time matches Eq. (4.2).

$$\max_{i}^{n}(t^i) \le t \le m \cdot (\sum_{i}^{n} t^i + p \cdot t_{\text{pen}}) \tag{4.2}$$

The t^i means the average maintaining time for the i-th service in the target collection of the maintaining task. And p is the possibility of failing maintenance with time penalty (t_{pen}).

- Availability. The availability (marked as A) that we introduced is the proportion of time a system is in a functioning condition in the watching period. More specifically, we define the availability (in Eq. (4.3)) of the system during the maintenance as being the ratio of a system's available time to the longest maintaining time (i.e., watching period). The symbol U in Eq. (4.3) means the combination of pending and reloading time instead of the sum of them since the pending and reloading operations might overlap during the transferring or deploying of other components.

$$A = 1 - \frac{\bigcup_i (t_p^i + t_r^i)}{\sum_i t^i} \tag{4.3}$$

From the two metrics, we can find that the better maintaining solution is usually completed within less maintaining time and with higher availability. To achieve that, we will do analysis for the different dependencies in the next sections. For evaluation convenience, we also introduce the Loss Rate, the ratio of failure requests to the total requests during the watching period. Actually, it denotes the inverse proportion to the availability.

4.2.2 *Dependencies in a Grid*

As mentioned in Section 4.1, service dependency is rather complicated in service-oriented grids. From the view of grid developers, each composite service always depends on a bunch of service components in some business logic. On the other hand, from the view of grid administrators, the correct deployment or maintenance of service components also depends on the target hosting containers. Based on the literature (Sangal *et al.*, 2005; Talwar *et al.*, 2005) and our experience (Qi *et al.*, 2007), we classify the dependencies into three main types.

• *Deployment Dependency*: The deployment of services always requires that other related ones were deployed to the target container in advance. In addition to that, the versioning problem during maintenance also drives us to focus more on the dependency between the pre-deploying components and deployed service components. In desktop systems, the Berkeley DB3 is taken to record the deployment dependencies for Linux's RPM (Mugler *et al.*, 2005). In a distributed computing environment, the scenarios include deployment of a service component (e.g. Wikipedia website) that requires a database component in a version (e.g. MySQL-server-4.0.20-0) pre-installed in the remote site for the initializing purpose. If the administrator ignores this dependency, the maintenance fails. As a special case, the configuring dependency discussed in the literature (Talwar *et al.*, 2005) is a part of the deployment dependency.

• *Invocation Dependency*: It represents a key feature of SOA that happens between composite services (Sangal *et al.*, 2005). We describe three kinds of invocation dependency as examples:

- AND-dependency describes the aggregating relation of other service components. The typical scenario is the executing system in a grid. The execution managers (e.g. Grid Resource Allocate and Management, GRAM (Foster, 2006)) are AND depending on the information systems (e.g. Monitoring and Discovery System, MDS (Foster, 2006)), data file-transfers (e.g. Reliable File Transferring service, RFT (Foster, 2006)), and some other system functional services.

- XOR-dependency means the replication relationship. It can be explained as switch-case logic in Java. The requests to the composite service will be delivered randomly to the dependent components. This dependency is popularly seen in today's data centers. For instance, the data metadata manager usually dispatches the requests to the Replica services.

- OR-dependency denotes that the requests to some composite services could be ignored according to specific conditions. This dependency can be mapped to the *try...catch...finally* logic in Java. For example, the cache service for the information system is the preferred option by the front end service. However, when reading the cache fails, the front end service tries dispatching to the real database querying. In this scenario, we say that the front end service OR-dependency on the cache service and database querying service.

• *Environment Dependency*: The maintenance for a service might jointly affect other services' maintenance in the same environment when some functional services are hosted by the same computational node. For example, the Data and the Info service have been deployed on the same container. Despite this, they are neither deployment nor invocation dependent on each other. When maintaining the Data service, the availability and throughput of the Info service are jointly affected due to the restarting container operation which is delivered by the maintenance to the Data service.

4.2.3 *Maintaining Solution and Dependencies*

In this section, we will demonstrate the metrics for the current solutions and approaches to distributed maintenance.

Until now, the most popular approaches for distributed maintenance are still built on the shell scripts (e.g. Bash shell or Perl scripts) and executed in serial. A typical system includes OSCAR (Mugler *et al.*, 2005), Beowulf (Headley and Mielke, 2005) and so on. With performance demands growing, the maintaining solution is being implemented in an advanced parallel program. The SmartFrog (Sabharwal, 2006) proposed by HP, ProActive (Baduel *et al.*, 2006) proposed by INRIA and MPICH-G2 (Karonis *et al.*, 2003) proposed by Globus Alliance are always adopted to implement the parallel maintenance toolkit. The two types of solutions have different features for maintaining time and availability.

• *Language-Based Maintenance in Parallel*: By using this solution, we can get the maintaining time easily if there are no considerations about the dependency.

$$t = \max_i^n (t^i) \tag{4.4}$$

In addition, the availability of the system based on the definition in Section 4.2.1 is as follows:

$$A = 1 - \frac{\max_{i=1}^n (t_r^i + t_p^i)}{\sum_{i=0}^n t^i} \tag{4.5}$$

However, if there is a deployment dependency, the availability will drop to zero and can't be recovered even after maintenance. The reason is that the failure of the deployment dependency crashes the maintenance to the depending service component while the dependent services are maintained as normal. The result is that the system will be unavailable forever.

On the other hand, this approach is also not acceptable for invocation dependencies (e.g. OR- and XOR-dependency), because whenever the composite service or its service components firstly finish maintenance, the availability of system is sacrificed.

• *Script-Based Maintenance in Serial*: As the other frequently used approach for the daily maintenance, this costs far more time to finish the maintenance (as shown in Eq. (4.6)).

$$t = \sum_i^m t^i \tag{4.6}$$

It provides the availability of

$$A = 1 - \frac{\sum_{i=0}^m (t_r^i + t_r^p)}{\sum_{i=0}^n t^i} \tag{4.7}$$

In Eq. (4.7), the *m* means the maintaining steps to be executed for *n* services. It shows that the availability during this solution is lower than the parallel.

Although the serial approach does not lead to a deployment dependency problem, it is not acceptable for most maintaining cases because of its poor availability and efficiency.

4.2.4   Objectives

Section 4.2.3 discusses the shortages of the traditional maintaining approaches with service dependencies. The motivation to build a highly available maintaining mechanism includes the following items:

• *Improve the Global Availability during the Maintenance*: The executions of upgrade, undeploy and deactivate tasks inevitably make some service components inaccessible. This definitely brings a chain reaction to the components that are invocation-dependent on them. The result lowers the availability of the global system. Similarly, the environment dependency is another factor to lower the availability of the global system. A grid needs a mechanism to balance global availability and the demands of maintenance.

• *Reduce the Possible Failures of Maintenance*: As discussed in Section 4.2.1, ignorance of deployment dependency always leads to failed maintenance. Especially in a highly distributed grid, the failure will be amplified to the whole system and eventually it will crash. The traditional maintaining approaches (e.g. manual, script and language-based by Talwar *et al.* (2005) can't resolve this well without handling the dependencies. On the other hand, when a service is being deployed or upgraded, the maintenance also fails if the target environment lacks its dependent service packages (i.e., environment dependency). To avoid that, a mechanism should be provided to find out these dependent components and deploy them first.

• *Improve the Efficiency of Maintenance*: As mentioned in Section 4.1, most of the maintaining tasks require propagating to the related computing resources in parallel to saving maintenance time. We try to find the optimized solution to balance concurrency and correctness when introducing the dependency factors.

4.3 Definitions

Definition 4.1 (Service Dependency) R is a binary relationship on S. We mark it as $s_i > s_j$. It has properties as follows:

• For any $s_i \in \dot{S}$, $\exists \dot{s}_i > s_j$. Namely, any service "depends on" itself by default. Hence dependency is reflexive;

• For any $s_i, s_j, s_k \in S$, whenever $s_i > s_j$, and $s_j > s_k$, we have $s_i \gg s_k$. This means dependency is transitive. To identify the direct and indirect dependency, we mark the latter relationship as $\gg$. Particularly, if $s_k = s_j$, we can get a cycle dependency $s_i \gg s_j$.

$S_{in}(s_i)$ and $S_{out}(s_i)$ are the sets of depended and depending (including direct and indirect) services for s_i respectively. For any two services in S, if they have the same depending and depended set, we call them isomorphic. The isomorphic services can be deployed concurrently or in the same package to the target sites.

Definition 4.2 (Direct Dependency Set) We define $\sum(s_i)$ as a direct dependency set for a proper service S_i in the whole VO. By exploring $\sum(S)$, we can draw a Directed Graph $DG\langle S, \sum(S)\rangle$ with the following properties:

• Each $s_i \in S$ is expressed as a vertex in DG;

• Each dependency candidate in $\sum$ is expressed as a directed edge.

In addition, we define $R_k(s_i)$ $(k > 0)$ as the k-th transitive dependency relationship for service s_i. Such as $R_3(s_i)$, its distance is three edges away from s_i. Furthermore, the symbol $\sum closure\ s(i)$ is the transitive closure for service s_i. Simply put, it means all the dependencies (including the indirect and the direct) for s_i. The operator $\bigcup$ in Formula (4.8) means the combination of the dependency sets.

Definition 4.3 (Critical Deployment Path) It is a minimal subset of $\sum(s_i)$ in which the edges can link all of the vertices that service s_i is depending on.

$$\sum(s_i) = \bigcup_{k=1}^{n} R^k(s_i), n = \|S\|, \ n > 0 \tag{4.8}$$

By exploring all the vertices (services) on this path, we can build a minimal deployment solution to promise correct deployment of service s_i.

Definition 4.4 (Service Dependency Matrix) Similar to Sangal *et al.* (2005), we define a Service Dependency Matrix (SDM) as an $n \times n$ mesh. Each element $d_{i,j}$ in the SDM matrix means the direct dependency relationship between s_i and s_j. As described in Eq. (4.9), the value of the i-th row and j-th column will be 1 if s_i depends on s_j. Otherwise, it will be 0.

$$d_{i,j} = \begin{cases} 1 & s_i > s_j \\ 0 & \text{else} \end{cases} \tag{4.9}$$

Furthermore, we define the service Depending Degree of a specific service as $DGD(s_i)$ which records how much does service s_i depend on other services (except itself). Similarly, we define the Depended Degree of a specific service as $DDD(s_j)$ which measures how much do other services (except itself) depend on it. The value of *DGD* and *DDD* are defined in Formulae (4.10) and (4.11).

$$DGD(s_i) = \begin{cases} 0, & n = 1 \\ \dfrac{1}{n-1} \left(\left\| SDM_i + SDM_i^2 + \cdots + SDM_i^n \right\| - 1 \right), & n > 1 \end{cases} \tag{4.10}$$

In Eq. (4.10), the SDM_i is the vector of i-th row in mesh SDM. The SDM_i^k denotes the k-th transition vector (Yau and Tsai, 1987). In addition to that, Operator+ is defined as Boolean OR for vectors. SDM^T is the transpose of the matrix *SDM*.

$$DDD(s_i) = \begin{cases} 0, & n = 1 \\ \dfrac{1}{n-1} \left(\left\| T_i + T_i^2 + \cdots + T_i^n \right\| - 1 \right), & n > 1 \end{cases}, \quad T_i = SDM^T \tag{4.11}$$

The value of *DDD* and *DGD* can give an external evaluation for a particular service.

Lemma 4.1 A graph $DG\langle S, \sum(S)\rangle$, and we have the $DDD(S)$ and $DGD(S)$ with the following properties:

    I. If there are no circuits on *DG*, then for any service $s_i \in S$, the summation of $DDD(s_j)$ and $DGD(s_j)$ should be less than 1.

    II. Otherwise, if there are one or more circuits in graph $DG\langle S, \sum(S)\rangle$, we can find at least two services of which the summation of *DDD* and *DGD* is greater than 1.

    III. More specifically, these service vertices are on the circuits.

Proof. Items I and II can be proved easily from the definition of *DDD* and *DGD*. A service on the circuit will be the depended vertex and depending vertex at the same time for other services on the circuit. It is counted twice respectively in *DDD* and *DGD*. Hence the summation of them will be greater than I.

For Item III we take the counter evidence: Suppose there is a service s_i which is not on any circuit and the summation of *DDD* and *DGD* is greater than I. From the former discussion, we can find that at least a service s_j is both in the depended set and the depending set of s_i. Namely, we have $s_i \gg s_j$ and $s_j \gg s_i$. Dependency is transitive, hence we have $s_i \gg s_i$. It denotes that s_i is on a circuit. This conflicts with the hypothesis. Hence the conclusion of Item III is true.

Lemma 4.2 If there is a circuit in graph $DG\langle S, \sum(S)\rangle$, for each service vertex on that circuit, the value of *DDD* (resp. *DGD*) is equal to each other. Namely, these vertices are isomorphic.

Proof. With the definition of isomorphic and *DDD*, *DGD*, it can be easily concluded that if any two services (s_i, s_j) in *DG* are isomorphic, then they should have the same *DDD* and *DGD*. Hence, we just need to prove that the services s_i and s_j are isomorphic. Because s_i and s_j are on the circuit, we have $s_i \gg s_j$ and $s_j \gg s_i$. For any s_k in $S_{out}(s_i)$ we have $s_i \gg s_k$. We can get $s_j \gg k_j$ easily. Hence, for any service existing in $S_{out}(s_i)$, it should be in $S_{out}(s_k)$. Vice versa, based on the reflexive feature, any service existing in $S_{out}(s_k)$ should be also in $S_{out}(s_i)$. Then services s_i and s_j have the same depending set. Similarly, we can prove that they have the same dependent set. Thus service s_i and s_j are isomorphic.

The conclusion of Lemma 4.2 is true.

Definition 4.5 (State Matrix) We define a State Matrix (SM) to record the necessary state value. There would be multiple SMs with the transformation of stateful services, e.g. the XOR-dependency, AND-dependency and so forth. The result of the Boolean operation (AND) between the original SDM and the SD will be a new SDM.

4.4   Design of Cobweb Guardian

In this section, we will demonstrate our design to shield the affects from various dependencies. First, we design a two-layer architecture to efficiently record dependencies automatically.

4.4.1   Architecture

As shown in Fig. 4.2, the two layers are the Cobweb Guardian (CG) and Atomic Guardian (AG). A CG communicates with multiple AGs to execute the maintenance instructions for a grid. It includes four main functional modules as follows:

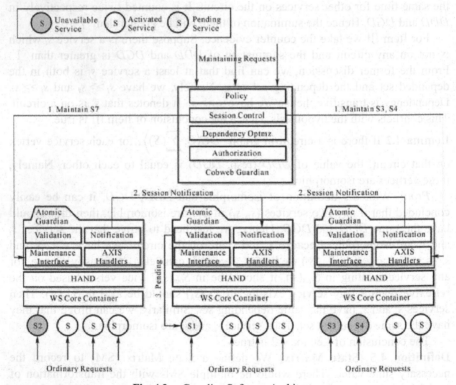

Fig. 4.2.   Guardian Software Architecture

(i) The session control module is mainly in charge of the progress of the maintenance. In addition, it also propagates the maintenance tasks to the replica of targets.

(ii) The dependency optimizer is the kernel of CG. It parses the input and matches the requirements against the existing dependency maps. The dependency map is designed as the dependency tables in MySQL database with version 5.0.33.

(iii) The authorization module is designed to check all of the maintenance requests to avoid unpredictable problems (e.g. requests to deploy Trojan viruses).

(iv) The policy module is designed for the administrator to execute on demand maintenance.

The Atomic Guardian, the actual maintainer, is implemented upon HAND infrastructure (Qi *et al.*, 2007). Similarly, AG consists of four parts:

(i) The notification module reports the maintenance states to dependent services and the Cobweb Guardian. With this module, administrators can grasp the progress of any maintenance and detect failures in the meantime. The notifications would only be sent to the peer which depends on the services under maintenance.

(ii) The validation module is the sink of the peer container's notification module. AG will execute pending commands or actions defined in policies to process the corresponded notifications.

(iii) Maintenance interface accepts the requests from the session control module. It actually executes the deploying, upgrading or activating of works by talking with the management module of the hosting container, i.e., HAND discussed in Chapter 3.

(iv) Axis handler implements Apache Axis (version 1.2) handler interface *invoke*() and it is designed to record the different invocation dependencies from the input and output message flow. Any recorded peers would be notified by the notification module during the maintenance. It efficiently helps CG reduce the overhead.

By implementing the two layers, the deployment dependencies can be recorded and administrated from CG, and the invocation dependencies can be correctly collected by the AG's handler. These dependencies can be aware of our provisioning architecture.

In the next sections, we will propose our solutions to optimize the maintenance procedure according to the recorded dependencies.

4.4.2 Environment Dependency-Aware Maintenance in Three Granularities

By resolving and analyzing the maintenance requests, CG adapts different granularities according to related environment dependencies. The efficient reduction of maintenance granularity can help improve the efficiency of maintenance. Three-layer architecture (as shown in Fig. 4.3) is proposed in Cobweb Guardian to reduce the effects of dependency hierarchy.

• *Service Level*: It exists as a manager in the target hosting environment. The service-level maintenance means that all of the maintaining tasks are isolated for the target service component. The reloading or pending operations are only executed as the unit of services. The other services in the same environment will not be affected.

• *Container Level*: It works in the hosting environment. Unlike service-level maintenance, the reloading or pending operations are for the whole container. Namely, if a service in a container needs maintenance, the other services are also put into the maintaining state. This level is implemented widely in current applications such as GT4, MySQL server and HTTPD server. Although the granularity of this level is bigger than the service-level, it can save much time when maintaining a bunch of service components once in the same container.

• *Node Level*: The maintenance at node level is from the global view. The reloading or pending operations in this level will issue a bunch of computing nodes. It balances the maintaining policies among the different containers. By communicating with the service and container-level maintenance manager separately (as shown in Fig. 4.3), it guarantees that optimized and safe maintaining solutions are adopted. For instance, the related maintenance can reduce the effects from the hosting environment.

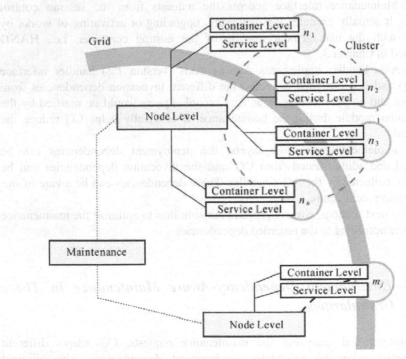

Fig. 4.3. Three-layer architecture for maintenance

4.4.3 Deployment Dependency-Aware Propagating Maintenance

Similar to the actions of RPM (Mugler *et al.*, 2005) manager in the Linux system, the CG will check this dependency before the maintenance and generate the critical maintaining path to propagate the operations. Namely, CG provides the session mechanism to guarantee the procedure of maintenance. The idea is from the parallel topological sorting algorithm (Kimelman and Zernik, 1993) and dynamical maintenance for k-connectivity Graph (Liang *et al.*, 2001). CG propagates the maintaining operations of depended service firstly to promise the maintenance can be executed correctly. If the propagations are finished in k steps, this solution will cost time of:

$$t = \sum_{i}^{k} \max_{j}^{s(i)} (t^j) \qquad (4.12)$$

The $s(i)$ in Formula (4.12) means the parallel maintenances for step i. And the availability is:

$$A = 1 - \sum_{i=0}^{k} (t_r^i + t_p^i) / \sum_{i=0}^{n} t_r \qquad (4.13)$$

It denotes that the maintenance time is longer than the simply parallel solution. However the correctness of maintenance is guaranteed. Fig. 4.4 demonstrates this procedure. Line 4 is to combine the possible maintenance from the deployment dependencies.

```
input  : (S × R)and the requested maintenance op. op is the maintenance for service s ∈ S
         (pre-)deployed on resource r ∈ R;
output: maintaining status

foreach (s,r) ∈ (S × R) do
    // invoke function GetDeployDependency to find out the
       deployment dependencies on resource r for service s.
    (Sr,op) ← GetDeployDependency(s,r);
    if Sr ≠ ∅ then
        // combine the deployment-depending tasks into task list
           to promise the correctness.
        manstack ← manstack ∪(Sr × {r},op);
    end
end
// sort the depending tasks and execute concurrently.
status ← ParallelExecute(TopologySort(manstack));
return status;
```

Fig. 4.4. Deployment dependency-aware maintenance algorithm

4.4.4   Invocation Dependency-Aware Grouping Maintenance

To achieve higher availability during maintenance, the different semantics of invocations are differentiated by the AG.
   • *For AND-dependency*: The maintenance for any service in this dependency

reduces the availability since the unavailability of any component can be transmitted in a chain to the whole system. The best solution is to propagate all of the maintenance to the target containers at the same time.

• *For XOR- and OR-dependency*: Because the ordinary requests are always dispatched to the composite services in a proper policy (e.g. round robin, random and load balancing policy), if the maintenance for composite services can be executed in groups, the availability can be improved to some extent. Eq. (4.14) describes the improved availability by using this approach. The p_i ($0<p_i<1$) in Eq. (4.14) means the possibility of dispatching requests to the maintaining containers. In addition, the t^0 means maintenance to the front end service component.

$$A = \left(1 - t_r^0 + t_p^0 + \sum_{i=1}^{k} p_i \cdot (t_r^i + t_p^i) \middle/ \sum_{i=0}^{n} t_i \right) \qquad (4.14)$$

However, the maintaining time is also increased since we add the groups in serial (the bigger k in Eq. (4.13)) for the maintenance. Fig. 4.5 is the process of grouping the target resources. From line 7 to 9 we can find that CG will group OR- and XOR-dependent service components and maintain them earlier (with a higher priority).

```
input : (S × R)and the requested maintenance op. op is the
        maintenance for service s ∈ S (pre-)deployed on resource r ∈ R;
output: maintaining status

 1 foreach (s, r) ∈ (S × R) do
       // invoke function GetInvokeDependency to find out the
          deployment dependencies on resource r for service s.
 2     (Sr, op) ← GetInvokeDependency(s,r);
 3     if Sr ≠ ∅ then
 4         switch TypeOf (Sr,s) do identify the type of invocations
 5             case AND dependency
                 | ;                        // do nothing for AND
 6             end
 7             case XOR- or OR-dependency
 8                 | manstack (Sr).priority ++ ;    // group the services
 9             end
10         end
11     end
12 end
    // sort the depending tasks and execute concurrently.
13 foreach each group do
14     status ← ParallelExecute(TopologySort(manstack),groupId);
15     if status = Failed then
16         | break;
17     end
18 end
19 return status;
```

Fig. 4.5. Invocation dependency-aware grouping maintenance algorithm

4.4.5 Grouping Maintenance with Feedback

Although the grouping solution improves the availability by sacrificing the maintaining time, it also brings unpredictable factors to the system. For instance, some critical invocations will be rejected randomly. The CG provides the feedback notification interface for the grid applications. By checking the status of the remote service components, the grid applications can bypass the requests to the maintaining service component. In this solution, the availability can be much improved. Actually, the cost is mainly from the maintenance of a composite service component.

$$A = 1 - \left((t_r^0 + t_p^0) \Big/ \sum_{i=0}^{n} t_i \right) \qquad (4.15)$$

Eq. (4.15) proved that the availability is better than serial, propagating and grouping maintenance solutions. Fig. 4.6 is similar to Fig. 4.5. It groups the depending services firstly. The difference (line 10 to 12) is that the CG will query the feedback status from the service components. If the remote service components are unavailable, the priority decreases to a lower level. Sequentially, the maintenance to those would be postponed.

```
input  : (S × R)and the requested maintenance op. op is the maintenance for service
         s ∈ S (pre-)deployed on resource r ∈ R;
output: maintaining status
 1  foreach (s,r) ∈ (S × R) do
        // invoke function GetInvokeDependency to find out the
           deployment dependencies on resource r for service
           s.
 2      (Sr, op) ← GetInvokeDependency (s,r);
 3      if Sr ≠ ∅ then
 4          switch TypeOf (Sr,s) do identify the type of invocations
 5              case AND dependency
                    | ;                          // do nothing for AND
 6              end
 7              case XOR or OR dependency
 8                  manstack (Sr).priority ++ ;   // group the services
 9                  foreach s ∈ Sr do
10                      if QueryFeedback (s,r) = unavailable then
11                          manstack (s).priority -- ;   // postpone the
                               maintenance.
12                      end
13                  end
14              end
15          end
16      end
17  end
        // sort the depending tasks and execute concurrently.
18  foreach each group do
19      status ← ParallelExecute (TopologySort (manstack).groupId);
20      if status = Failed then
21          break;
22      end
23  end
24  return status;
```

Fig. 4.6. Invocation dependency-aware grouping maintenance with feedback algorithm

4.5   Evaluations

We experimented with our implementation on the ChinaGrid test bed. Services in our experiments are evaluated on the ChinaGrid Support Platform v 2.0.1 (Wu *et al.*, 2005).

Our evaluation has the following objectives:

• To demonstrate the improved availability by comparing the traditional maintenance approach with our Cobweb Guardian.

• To compare the availability and throughput of different maintenance solutions of the Cobweb Guardian when the maintenance happened in different dependencies.

• To demonstrate the effectiveness of dependency feedback and different granularity of maintenance in improving the service availability and the throughput.

4.5.1   Test Environment

Unless otherwise stated, experiments in this chapter were conducted on two rack-mounted Linux clusters. One is with 16 nodes (each with 1.0 GHz Pentium III CPU and 512 MB memory). Each node runs Red Hat Linux with kernel version 2.4.20-8. The Java runtime version is J2SDK 1.5.0_06-b05 implemented by SUN. The other one employs 20 dual 1.3 GHz Itanium2 servers. The nodes inside the cluster are connected by a 100 Mbps Ethernet switch. Each node runs Red Hat Linux with kernel version 2.4.0-2. The Java runtime version is J2SDK 1.5.0_03-b07 implemented by BEA. The two clusters are also connected with bandwidth 100 Mbps.

To support the correct execution of the test case, it is necessary that the MPICH (version 1.2.4) and image processing toolkits have been deployed to the target systems in advance.

• *Abbreviations*: Here is a list of the abbreviations that we will use in the rest of this section:

- NonD denotes the normal maintaining solution in parallel, like ProActive or SmartFrog, without dependency consideration;

- SRL is to maintain the services by calling shell scripts in serial;

- CG-0 is the simple deployment dependency-aware propagating solution without optimization for invocation dependency;

- CG-1 means the invocation dependency-aware grouping maintenance;

- CG-2 is the grouping maintenance with feedback;

- REQ in the diagrams denotes the fixed requesting rates for particular service components.

• *Application for Benchmark*: Our experiments are running on a typical executing system, called General Running Service (GRS, S1), implemented by

CGSP. As shown in Fig. 4.7, the GRS includes 6 service components: authentication service (Auth, S2), information service (Info, S3), data management service (Data, S4), cache service (Cache, S5), collecting service (Collect, S6) and replication service (Replica, S7). The executing job issued in our experiment is an MPI-based image processing application (Haifang *et al.*, 2005) which is encapsulated and deployed in our ChinaGrid test bed. When a job request arrives, GRS parses it and then contacts the Auth component to check the validity, the Info component to get job's executing information and the Data component to fetch the staging data respectively. More particularly, the Info component will fetch the job information from the Cache first. If it fails then invokes the Collect to query in a backend database. On the other hand, the Data adopts a replication to store and load the staging data (a sample image). There can be multiple partitions for the Info and the GRS. The detailed semantics of CGSP's execution system can be investigated in the literature (Wu *et al.*, 2005). By injecting the maintenances to these services, we can inspect the capability of Cobweb Guardian.

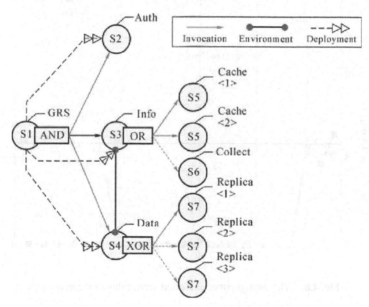

Fig. 4.7. Service dependencies in CGSP's execution system

4.5.2 Deployment Dependency-Aware Propagation

To investigate the efficiency of the propagation feature and the effects of deployment dependency, we drive the GRS service at 6 requests per second in this experiment. We run the experiment for 140 s. At second 15, we inject the maintenance to the GRS (including upgrades of Auth, Info, Data service components and itself) which then becomes unresponsive for a while. Three solutions have been tested (i.e., NonD, SRL and CG-0) in this experiment.

Fig. 4.8 shows the throughput of the three solutions during the 30-second watching period. When there was no maintenance, all systems worked well. When maintenance started at second 15, the throughputs of the system with different approaches were all falling to zero. Although the NonD solution finished the maintenance earliest, it could not work correctly any more. Because it did not consider the deployment dependencies between service components, the maintenance for the GRS component failed finally. Although the SRL solution finished maintenance correctly, it cost too much time. Against the two solutions, CG-0 provides the highest efficiency. It lost 49.1% of requests since the AND-dependent service components are unavailable when any related service (i.e., Auth, Info and Data) is under maintenance.

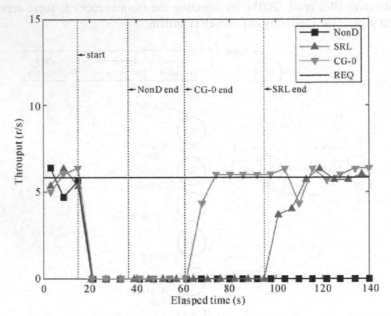

Fig. 4.8.   The throughput of execution service during the maintenance

4.5.3 Invocation Dependency-Aware Grouping

In the next two experiments, we take the Info service to evaluate the effectiveness of CG for improving service availability in different invocation-dependencies. We drive the system at 10 requests per second to Info service.

  • *OR-dependency*: As shown in Fig. 4.9, at second 15 we started maintaining solutions CG-0 and CG-1 respectively. CG-0 propagated the maintaining tasks to the target containers that deployed the Cache and Collect service components and then to the nodes with the Info service. The whole procedure cost 62.97 s. However, from Table 4.1, we can find that the throughput during the execution of CG-0 was falling near to zero. In addition to that, there are 57.9% requests that were lost in the watching period (defined in Section 4.2).

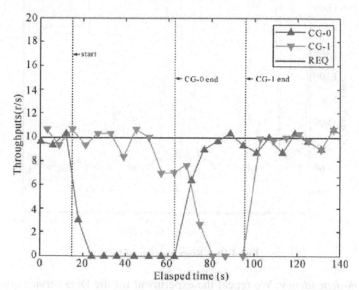

Fig. 4.9. Throughput of Info

Table 4.1 Comparison of experimental results

Approaches	Maintenance	Response time (ms)	Throughput	Loss ratio (%)
CG-0	Before	443.9	9.51	0
	During	N/A	0.86	57.9
CG-1	Before	463.8	9.92	0
	During	929.8	7.08	25.6

As in the comparison with CG-0, the CG-1 optimized the solution for OR-dependency. The CG maintained the target containers in sequence with the different priorities. The improvement is obvious: First, the throughput during the maintenance is improved to 7.08 requests per second. Although the average response time is 929.8 ms which is about double that before maintenance, the loss ratio reduces from 57.9% to 25.6%. Meanwhile, the 25.6% is the minimum cost for all solutions because the maintenance for the Info service is the key maintenance which is hard to avoid. From Fig. 4.9, we can identify that the throughput of CG-1 falls to about 7.3 from second 57 because the requests to the Cache services failed when they were under maintenance. Thus the requests were sent to the Collect service forcedly.

Fig. 4.10 denotes the response time for the procedures mentioned above. We can easily find that the average response time increases when the Cache service begins to be maintained (at second 57). The improvement is acceptable against solution CG-0. However, the improvement in CG-1 sacrificed the maintaining time. We have to take 32.985 s to finish the maintenance job.

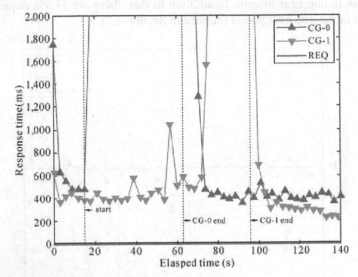

Fig. 4.10.   Response time of Info

• *XOR-dependency*: We repeat the experiment for the Data service component (XOR-dependency). This time we introduce solution CG-2. This maintenance solution feeds back the maintaining status to the user-level application. According to the status, these services take some strategies to avoid mistaken accesses to the services that are under maintenance. Similarly, we started the three maintenances at second 15 respectively.

Fig. 4.11 describes the whole procedure: The CG-0 solution acted as before. It blocked all of the requests to the Data service during the maintenance. Hence the throughput for CG-0 is the lowest. However the CG-1 solution did not act well either. Although it improved the throughput to some extent (from 0 to 4.71), the loss rate was about 52.1% which was a minor improvement to the CG-0's 53.9%. The main reason is that the CG-1 cost more time to finish the maintenance than the CG-0. Otherwise, the Data service was always trying to deliver requests to the Replicas service during the maintenance. These requests failed definitely. Unlike the CG-0 and CG-1, solution CG-2 worked far better. It cost the same time to finish maintenance like the CG-0. However, it gave better throughput (6.56), lower loss rate (25.9%) and better response time for normal requests (478 ms). Table 4.2 lists the average response time, throughput and loss rate respectively for the three solutions at different stages, both before and during maintenance. It reflects the variations discussed above.

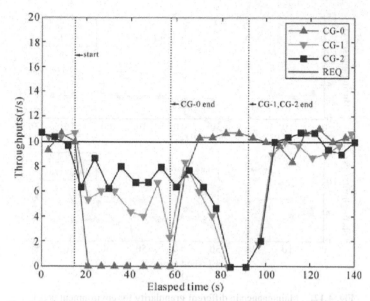

Fig. 4.11.   The throughput of the virtual data center service during the maintenance

Table 4.2   Comparison of experimental results

Approaches	Maintenance	Response time (ms)	Throughput	Loss ratio (%)
CG-0	Before	552.5	9.21	0
	During	N/A	0.01	53.9
CG-1	Before	405.6	9.43	0
	During	933.2	4.71	52.1
CG-2	Before	405.1	10.07	0
	During	478.5	6.56	25.9

4.5.4   Environment Dependency-Aware Maintenance in Different Granularities

To demonstrate the enhancement of environment dependency, we executed the upgrade for the Info service component that was deployed with the Data service component in the same container.

Fig. 4.12 describes the results. Fig. 4.12(a) denotes container-level maintenance and Fig. 4.12(b) is in the service-level. As shown in Fig. 4.12, in the container-level maintenance, the Data service was also unavailable when Info service was under upgrading. However, the maintenance in the service-level did not affect the access to the Data service. In addition to that, the maintenance time in the service-level (14.6 s) was also shorter than the container-level (23.6 s). This result proved that the availabilities for the Data and the Info service components were enhanced.

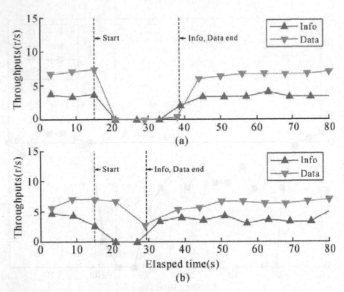

Fig. 4.12.   Maintenance in different granularity for environment dependency

4.5.5   *Evaluation for Dynamicity*

According to the realistic statistics in Section 4.1, the biggest convenience for VO users is completing the admin maintenances for the infrastructure transparently and efficiently. In this experiment, we investigate the effectiveness for dynamical variation which is very common for grid services. Besides the normal maintenance (transfer the upgrading packages, reload the hosting container and so on) for the Data and its Replica services, an un-deployment is executed for one of its replica.

The CG-1 solution is used in this experiment. Fig. 4.13 depicts the throughput's variation for this maintenance. From Fig. 4.13, we can find out that after the whole maintenance the throughput fell to 2/3 of the original throughput before the maintenance. This proved that the Replica service was un-deployed successfully. In addition, the throughputs were lowered in three stages during the maintenance procedure since the Cobweb Guardian blocked the requests to the service components which were under maintenance. Meanwhile, the loss ratio during maintenance is 25.7%. It is near to the minimum value.

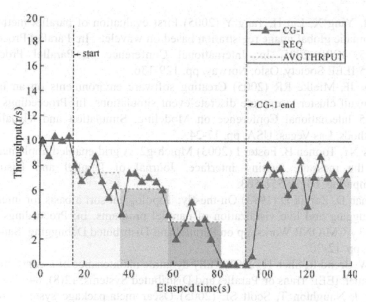

Fig. 4.13. Throughput variance when dynamically changing the services

4.6 Summary

In this chapter, we propose the Cobweb Guardian which is a dependency-aware maintenance architecture for service-oriented grids. By investigating the effects of the different dependencies in the runtime of the grid (including invocation, deployment and environment-dependency), the Cobweb Guardian can automatically generate the optimized solutions for maintenance in distributed grids. The evaluations demonstrate the effectiveness of the Cobweb Guardian in improving availability and throughput during the maintenance.

References

Baduel L, Baude F, Caromel D, Contes A, Huet F, Morel M, Quilici R (2006) Programming, deploying, composing for the Grid. In: Cunha JC, Rana OF (eds.) Grid Computing: Software Environments and Tools. Springer-Verlag, New York, USA, pp. 205-229.

Foster I (2006) Globus toolkit version 4: Software for service-oriented systems. Journal of Computer Science and Technology, 21(4): 513-520.

Foster I, Kesselman C, Tuecke S (2001) The anatomy of the grid: Enabling scalable virtual organizations. International Journal of High Performance Computing Applications, 15(3): 200-222.

Zhou H, Yang X, Liu H, Tang Y (2005) First evaluation of parallel methods of automatic global image registration based on wavelets. In: Parallel Processing, 2005. ICPP 2005. In: International Conference on Parallel Processing 2005.IEEE Society, Oslo, Norway, pp. 129-136.

Headley JF, Mielke RR (2005) Creating software environments on an m-node Beowulf cluster to execute discrete-event simulations. In: Proceedings of the 2005 International Conference on Modeling, Simulation and Visualization Methods. Las Vegas, USA, pp. 17-24.

Karonis NT, Toonen B, Foster I (2003) Mpich-g2: A grid-enabled implementation of the message passing interface. Journal of Parallel and Distributed Computing, 63(5): 551-563.

Kimelman D, Zernik D (1993) On-the-fly: Topological sort a basis for interactive debugging and live visulization of parallel programs. In: Proceedings of the 1993 ACM/ONR Workshop on Parallel and Distributed Debugging. San Diego, CA, pp. 12-20.

Liang W, Brend R, Shen H (2001) Fully dynamic maintenance of k-connectivity in parallel. IEEE Trans on Parallel and Distributed Systems, 12(8): 846 864.

Mugler J, Naughton T, Scott SL (2005) Oscar meta-package system. In: 19th International Symposium on High Performance Computing Systems and Applications, 2005. HPCS 2005, IEEE Computer Society, Guelph, Ontario, Canada, pp. 353-360.

Qi L, Jin H, Foster I, Gawor J (2007) Hand: Highly available dynamic deployment infrastructure for globus toolkit 4. In: Vecchia GD, di Serafino D, Marra I, Perla F (eds.) 15th Euromicro International Conference on Parallel, Distributed and Network-Based Processing (PDP 2007). IEEE Computer Society, Naples, Italy, pp. 155-162.

Sabharwal R (2006) Grid infrastructure deployment using smartfrog technology. In: Bader DA, Khokhar AA (eds.) International Conference on Networking and Services, 2006. IEEE Computer Society, Washington, DC, USA, pp. 73-73.

Sangal N, Jordan E, Sinha V, et al. (2005) Using dependency models to manage complex software architecture. In: Gabriel RP (ed.) International Conference on Object Oriented Programming, Systems, Languages and Applications 2005. IEEE Computer Society, San Diego, USA, pp. 167-176.

Talwar V, Milojicic D, Wu Q (2005) Approaches for service deployment. IEEE Internet Computing, 9(2): 70-80.

Wu Y, Wu S, Yu H, Hu C (2005) Cgsp: An extensible and reconfigurable grid framework. In: Yang LT (ed.) The 6th International Workshop on Advanced Parallel Processing Technologies, Springer, Hong Kong, China, pp. 292-300.

Yau S, Tsai J (1987) Knowledge representation of software component interconnection information for large-scale software modifications. IEEE Transactions on Software Engineering, SE-13(3): 355-342.

5

Asynchronous Provisioning Strategy for Heterogeneous Grids

Abstract: Following upon the infrastructure and architecture discussed in the former chapters, this chapter proposes a distributed and asynchronous model in our Guardian maintenance system for dynamic provisioning that is well-suited to such an intricate setting. The solution introduces multiple maintaining layers so that all the maintenance instructions can be done in an asynchronous way. Experimenting with the new model, in which maintenances are executed in an interlaced time sequence, the downtime of the global system during service maintenance can be effectively reduced by preventing a Weakest Link Effect usually arising from individual heterogeneity or emergent faults. Thus, the consistency of alien nodes and the execution of new requests (after maintenance) can be guaranteed simultaneously. In particular, the implications of maintenance due to heterogeneous dependencies can be detected and resolved automatically in this framework. The practical evaluations prove that the Guardian system equipped with this model can improve the availability and reduce downtime effectively.

5.1   Motivation

Federated computing infrastructures such as computational grids (Foster and Kesselman, 1998) have the potential to provide high assurance for data-intensive or computation-intensive applications such as Web service composition, distributed stream processing and workflow management. As these computing infrastructures continue to grow, how to efficiently manage such large-scale dynamic distributed systems to better support potentially unbounded user needs has become a challenging problem.

As discussed in Chapter 1, heterogeneity and fault tolerance bring far more troubles to distributed maintenance. Because a part of various grid services is deployed on large-scale distributed resources, maintenance suffers from high inconsistency and complicated dependencies. First, the administrator has to consider the various maintaining tasks for heterogeneous resources (e.g. the installation packages for Linux and Windows). Second, he has to find all possible implicational maintenances to resolve the heterogeneity of services (e.g. compliance among different versions). Finally, he should consider how to reduce the inconsistency caused by emergent faults and continue the paused maintenances correctly. These factors of inconsistency bring us a big challenge: Which resource in the maintaining list is the slowest for maintenance of the grid and how to reduce its impact on the global system? Similar to Salemie (2006) who addressed the impact of a Wide Area Network (WAN) on the performance of networking applications, we call this inconsistency of maintenance the Weakest Link Effect. Although many studies (Jin *et al.*, 2007; Qi *et al.*, 2007a; Sabharwal, 2006; Shwartz *et al.*, 2005; Talwar *et al.*, 2005; Zielinski *et al.*, 2005) have investigated different architectures for maintenance of scalable and distributed computational systems, these solutions focus on resolving the scalability, availability or usability challenges. They can't handle the Weakest Link Effect problem. In this chapter, we concentrate on how to reduce this impact from heterogeneity and transient failures.

We explore a new design dimension, i.e., provide a distributed and asynchronous model, to intelligently maintain the grid system with a minimum overhead. By introducing asynchronous maintenance for distributed computational resources, a new Guardian service can execute the related maintenance dynamically upon the demands of users and the status of target resources. Besides the enhanced efficiency, the new model brings a better capability of handling heterogeneity and transient failures during the maintenance. Naturally it promises correctness of applications without modifying any codes.

5.2   Asynchronous Provisioning Model

To resolve the problems addressed in Section 5.1, we introduce a novel asynchronous provisioning model. The new model includes a set of definitions and specifications as following.

5.2.1   Traditional Maintaining Solutions

As a traditional solution, Sync Maintenance is adopted by major maintaining workflow systems or virtual managing systems to propagate the daily maintaining instructions for a distributed environment.

In this way, for each maintenance, the maintaining module transfers the related configurations or packages to remote resources first, and then executes the maintaining operation. After finishing all the maintenance on the targets, it executes the next maintenance in the scripts or workflows. Normally the maintenance time is decided by package transferring time and actual execution time of each maintenance. The two factors are unpredictable due to an unstable network bandwidth, the processing capability of target resources and the availability of target resources. In particular, it can't guarantee consistency when emergencies happen. For example, some resources could be shut down and unavailable for several days when deploying a service. The whole maintenance will fail eventually due to this timeout. Although the policy solution (Shankar *et al.*, 2006) can reduce the affects of some specific emergencies (e.g. file transfer mistakes, maintenance failure and so on) to some extent, it can't handle all of the emergencies (e.g. long-term networking traffic jam). To remedy these shortages, the design of our system is motivated by the following goals:

• To avoid possible crashes from complicated dependencies and heterogeneity, the maintenance system should have the ability to tolerate possible emergencies and the heterogeneity brought by hardware and software (i.e., dependency hierarchy).

• To achieve the least downtime and the capability for transient tolerance, the maintenance system should provide a mechanism to guarantee each maintenance is executed in each target resource safely and robustly.

• To achieve the correct time sequence for the global system, the maintenance system should provide a mechanism to promise that the relative sequences between ordinary requests and maintenance requests are strictly identical.

5.2.2 Definitions for Asynchronous Maintenance

Motivated by the factors described in Section 5.1, we design the asynchronous and distributed maintaining model. The processes issued in maintenance are classified into three disjoint types: (i) a set $C = \{c_1, c_2, \cdots, c_k\}$ of client processes (client-tier) that deliver the ordinary and maintenance tasks randomly upon the demands of users; (ii) a set $M = \{m_1, m_2, ..., m_l\}$ of maintenance workers that respond to the maintenance requests from clients, plan the procedure and redirect the maintenance operations to the related resources; (iii) a set $R = \{r_1, r_2, \cdots, r_m\}$ of end computational resources that really execute the maintenance and functions defined by the service components.

Definition 5.1 (Service Component) A service component is defined as $s_i = \langle F_i, Imp, SD_i, DD_i \rangle$, where F_i represents the provided service functions, *Imp* defines the implementations of the service, *SD* represents the static data (i.e., configurations, endpoint location and deployment descriptor) and *DD* represents dynamic data (i.e., the runtime parameters, the staging data and the QoS demands).

In particular, in the service-oriented computing category, a service component is a self-contained software unit which provides a certain functionality (e.g. image processing, language translation and data encryption). Each service component has several input and output ports which are defined as Web Service Description Language (WSDL) for receiving the input parameters (or data) and sending out the results respectively.

Definition 5.2 (Maintenance Task) A maintenance task is an operational request from a user or an administrator (defined as $\Pi_{id} = \langle TS, R, OP \rangle$), where id means its global and unique sequence number, TS is the collection of services under maintenance, R represents the planned computational nodes related to the target service components and OP is the collection of maintenance operations such as deploy, backup, re-configure and so forth. Compared with the maintenance task, the ordinary requests (defined as $req(s_i, r_i)$) are the requests to the existing normal functional service component s_i which is deployed on the end resource r_i.

Definition 5.3 (Atomic Maintenance) An atomic maintenance is an atomic operational procedure which will be running physically on a specific resource (defined as $\tau_{id}^{r_k}(s_i, op)$), where id denotes the sequence number on resource r_k. It is unique for target resource r_k. This is different to the id defined in maintaining task. s_i is the service component that will be maintained. The atomic maintenance is decoupled from the maintenance task defined in Definition 5.2.

Definition 5.4 (Service Dependency $s_i \gtrless s_j$) Given two service components s_i and s_j, we define $s_i \gtrless s_j$ iff (1) $\exists f_a \in F_i$ needs invoking $f_b \in F_j (f_a^{s_i} \to f_b^{s_j})$ or (2) $SD_i \cap SD_j \neq \varnothing$.

In Definition 5.4, $SD_i \cap SD_j \neq \varnothing$ means that service s_i and s_j are installed on the same computational resource. Hence, we call the dependencies match condition one as invocation dependency and the other as environment dependency respectively (see Chapter 4). Due to the existence of the complicated dependencies, many invisible actions should be done when triggering a maintenance. As an example, we plan deploying a POVRay service (an image processing application) on the server r_a. If there is no data transferring component on r_a, the deployment will have to request deploying data transfer the component implicatively first. Accordingly, we define the implicational maintenance relationship as follows:

Definition 5.5 (Implicational Maintaining Relationship $\Pi_a^{TS_i} \in \Pi_b^{TS_j}$) Given two maintenance tasks $\Pi_a^{TS_i}$ and $\Pi_b^{TS_j}$, we define $\Pi_a^{TS_i}$ is $\Pi_b^{TS_j}$'s implicational task iff: (1) $\forall s_m \in TS_i, \exists s_n \in TS_j \to s_n \mu s_m$, (2) $TS_i \cap TS_j = \varnothing$, (3) $R_i \subseteq R_j$, (4)$b > a$.

Definition 5.5 describes the possible hidden maintenances (i.e., $\Pi_a^{TS_i}$) that should be done first (i.e., $b>a$) for specific resources R_i. The implicational maintenance should be automatically explored by the specific modules in the Guardian services.

Definition 5.6 (Query Task μ) A query task is a querying procedure from a computational resource $r \in R$ to the Guardian worker $m \in M$ (defined as $\mu_{id} = \langle s_j, r_p \rangle$), where id means the max sequence number for the requested service stored in the resource r_p and s_j is the service that needs to know the maintenance states.

Normally, the return of μ_{id} is the sequence number stored in the Guardian workers that are scheduled by the Guardian system. If the requested tasks are not planned, the returned value of μ will be null.

Definition 5.7 (Weakest-Link Effect) For a maintenance task $\Pi_a^{TS_i}$, $\forall s_k \in TS_i, \Pi_x^{\{sk\}} \in \Pi_a^{TS_i}$ is s_k's parallel division on target resources R, x is its scheduled sequence. Naturally the maintenance time of $\Pi_x^{\{sk\}}$ is $\max\limits_{r_k \in R} t_{r_{id}^k (s_k, op)}$, t_τ denotes the maintenance time of task τ. The weakest-link effect denotes that maintenance time $t_{\Pi_x^{\{sk\}}}$ will be postponed, largely due to the heterogeneity of maintenance targets and transient faults.

5.2.3 Specification

A correct implementation of the asynchronous model in the Guardian service must satisfy the specification of Specs 1 to 5 described below.

Spec 1 (Correctness of Termination) If a Guardian worker m_i is correct, $\tau_{id}()$ and $\mu_{id}()$ will return the correct results of a maintenance.

Furthermore, the following specifications should be guaranteed for the correct maintenance in the distributed environment.

Spec 2 (Uniform Agreement) If a Guardian worker $m_i \in M$ executes $\tau_p^{r_k}(s_k, op)$ $(1 \le p \le \infty)$, then all correct Guardian workers in M will eventually roll the states to $\tau_p^{r_k}(s_k, op)$.

Spec 3 (Uniform Integrity) $\forall r_i \in R$, every Guardian worker $m_i \in M$ executes $\tau_p^{r_i}(s_k, op)$ at most once.

Spec 4 (Uniform Maintaining Order) If $\Pi_{id+k} \cap \Pi_{id} = p$, $k \ge 0$ and $P \ne \emptyset$, then $\forall \tau_{id'}^r \in P$ should follow the sequence defined in Π_{id}. In particular, $\forall m_i \in M$ can't execute $\tau_{id'+1}$ if it has not previously executed $\tau_{id'}$ on resource r. The id' mentioned here means the actual sequence ID for the maintenance in a target resource.

Spec 5 (Correctness of Normal Request) Once a maintenance task $\Pi_{id}(TS, R, OP)$ has been submitted in time t, $\forall s_i \in TS$, any requests to s_i after t should be executed in the states of Π_{id}.

The Uniform Agreement (Spec 2) guarantees that two Guardian workers can't execute different maintenances for the same maintaining request; the Uniform

Integrity Property (Spec 3) avoids a Guardian worker executing the same atomic maintenance for the two distinct maintenance tasks. Furthermore, the Uniform Maintaining Order Property (Spec 4) guarantees the invoked atomic maintenances strictly follow the delivering sequence, i.e., the newly arrived maintenance should follow the historical sequence instead of the sequence defined in a new maintaining task. Finally, the Correctness of Normal Request (Spec 5) guarantees the correctness of the higher business logic. Namely, the normal requests to concrete resources after a maintenance should identically return the result from the maintained service component instead of the older one.

5.3   Maintenance Algorithms

In this section we introduce the implementation details of the asynchronous model. To guarantee the specifications discussed in Section 5.2.3, we implement the model as two important components: the virtual maintainer (act as *vm*) and some Guardian workers (act as m_i) in the mid-tier layer and an HAND handler (act as r_i) in the end-tier layer. Currently the model is implemented in the Guardian service of the ChinaGrid Support Platform version 2.0.2 (see Chapter 2).

5.3.1   The Virtual Maintainer

The pseudocode of the virtual maintainer is shown in Fig. 5.1. When the maintenance task is submitted from the administrating client, the virtual maintainer will check the service dependencies first, find out the implicational maintaining tasks and the allocated task stack (from line 2 to 15) for each service. By invoking the topology sorting algorithm (Gross and Tucker, 2001; Qi *et al.*, 2007b), the virtual maintainer decouples the maintenance task into several atomic maintenances. It pushes these atomic maintenances into the maintaining stack (line 20) of related resources and updates the sequence number of each maintenance (line 19). Fig. 5.2 demonstrates a heuristic scenario.

The maintenance task Π_i tries to deploy the service component s_1 to the resources r_1, r_2 and r_3. When the task is delivered to the virtual maintainer, the virtual maintenance algorithm finds out that due to the dependencies and heterogeneity there are two more atomic maintenances that should be executed before deploying s_1 to r_1. Therefore the task Π_i is decoupled into the atomic maintenances. Subsequently they are pushed into the maintaining stack of r_1, r_2 and r_3 respectively. In particular the sequence number of r_1, r_2 and r_3 is increased to $a+3$, $b+1$ and $c+1$ where a, b and c are the number of latest atomic maintenances in the maintaining stack of r_1, r_2 and r_3 respectively. Since service s_1 has been deployed before, there is only one atomic maintenance (τ_{*+1} for s_1)

delivered to r_2 and r_3 respectively. '*' is the local maintaining sequence number in r_2 and r_3.

```
input : Π_id(TS,R,OP).
output: Maintenance stack for resources ManStack

 1  foreach r_i ∈ R do
 2      foreach s_i ∈ TS_{r_i} do
 3          foreach f_i ∈ F^{s_i} do
 4              if f_i → f_k(f_k ∈ F^{s_p}) then
 5                  TS_{r_i} ← TS_{r_i} ∪ {s_p};
 6                  dependency ← dependency ∪ {s_i ≽ s_p};
 7              end
 8          end
 9          foreach sd_i ∈ SD^{s_i} do
10              if sd_i ∈ SD^{s_p} then
11                  TS_{r_i} ← TS_{r_i} ∪ {s_p};
12                  dependency ← dependency ∪ {s_i ≽ s_p};
13              end
14          end
15      end
16      TS_{ri} ← TopologySort (TS_{r_i},dependency);
17      foreach s_i ∈ TS_{r_i} do
18          if μ(s_i,r_i) = null then
19              id ← GetMax (r_i) +1;
20              manstack [r_i] ← manstack [r_i] ∪ τ_id(s_i,op);
21              broadcast τ_id to M;
22          end
23      end
24  end
25  return manstack;
```

Fig. 5.1. Asynchronous maintaining algorithm

More specifically, the maintenances stored in maintaining stacks are classified into three types as shown in Fig. 5.2.

• The *Finished* are the maintenances that have been correctly executed by Guardian workers on the resources;

• The *Executing* are the maintenances that are issued by some Guardian workers currently for correct execution of concrete service s_i;

• The *Planned* are the maintenances that have been decoupled and pushed into the maintenance stack by the virtual maintainer but not issued by the Guardian workers.

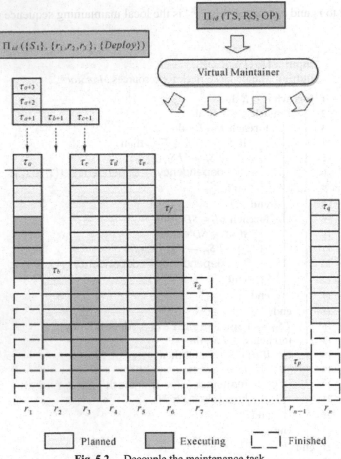

Fig. 5.2.   Decouple the maintenance task

5.3.2   *HAND Handler*

After pushing the atomic maintenances into the maintenance stack, these maintenances will not be executed immediately. Namely, they are not executed synchronously. By using the HAND mechanism discussed in Chapter 2, we deployed a handler on each resource that will decide when to trigger the maintenance according to respective status. The pseudocode of the HAND handler is presented in Fig. 5.3. Actually, when the ordinary requests arrive, this handler catches the SOAP message and judges the current states of the service container. If the requested service is available, the HAND handler will execute a querying task μ (line 7) to get the maximum maintaining sequence number of service s_i on resource r_i. If the sequence number (*currentId*) in the maintenance stack is greater than the *localId*, it means that a group of atomic maintenances are not yet executed. The handler will request the Guardian service to allocate a corresponding Guardian worker (line 11) m_i to execute the maintenances stored in the maintaining stack one by one (line 10 to line 18). Naturally, for the end of each maintenance, the *localId* will be updated to the corresponding sequence number. Meanwhile, if the maintenance refers to another dependent service (e.g. s_p), the status of s_p will be set to *unavailable* too. When all of the maintenances are finished, the HAND handler will dispatch the request to the instances of the specific service component physically (line 24). In this way, the Guardian service promises the execution of each ordinary request or maintaining request is correct and on-demand. A later section will formally prove the correctness. Fig. 5.4 describes the whole procedure by introducing the heuristic case. When a request for s_1 is delivered to the target resource r_1, the *currentId* of the maintenance stack will be returned by $\mu(s_1, r_1)$. The requested Guardian worker m_1 will fetch the atomic maintenances (from $\tau_{localId+1}$ to τ_μ) and execute them one by one on the resource r_1. After the maintenance, the normal requests will be processed correctly.

input : The ordinary request *req* from client to (s_i, r_i).
output: The response to client *resp*

```
1  while req arrived do
2  |   if status_{s_i} = maintaining then
3  |   |   resp ← 'service unavailable';
4  |   end
5  |   else
6  |   |   localId ← LocalMax(r_i);
7  |   |   currentId ← μ(s_i, r_i);
8  |   |   if currentId > localId then
9  |   |   |   status_{s_i} ← maintaining;
10 |   |   |   for k ← localId+1 to curentId do
11 |   |   |   |   (τ_k(s_p, op), m_p) ← GetGuard(k, r_i);
12 |   |   |   |   status_{s_p} ← maintaining;
13 |   |   |   |   m_p.run(τ_k);
14 |   |   |   |   localId_{s_p} ← k;
15 |   |   |   |   if s_p ≠ s_i then
16 |   |   |   |   |   status_{s_p} ← available;
17 |   |   |   |   end
18 |   |   |   end
19 |   |   end
20 |   |   else if currentId < localId then
21 |   |   |   RecoveryTo(currentId);
22 |   |   end
23 |   |   status_{s_i} ← available;
24 |   |   resp ← execute req;
25 |   end
26 |   return resp;
27 end
```

Fig. 5.3. Ordinary execution in end-tier

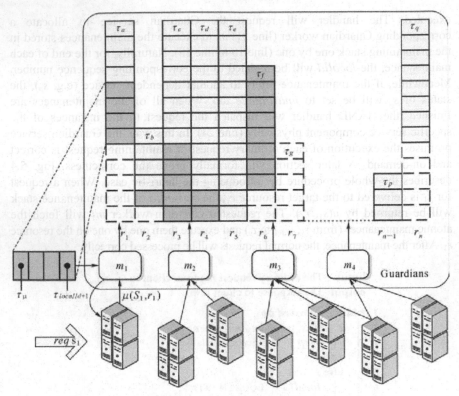

Fig. 5.4.   Execution of μ in end-tier

5.4   Time Sequence Analysis

We take an example (as shown in Fig. 5.5) to demonstrate the whole procedure. In this scenario, the client c_1 delivers maintaining task Π to maintain the service s_1 deployed on resources r_1, r_2 and r_3. When the maintaining task Π is delivered to the virtual maintainer (vm in Fig. 5.5), it analyzes the states of the related resources (i.e., r_1, r_2 and r_3) and finds out that there is an implicational maintenance, i.e., Π s_2, r_1, $deploy \in \Pi$ s_1, r_1, r_2, r_3, $deploy$, should be executed on r_1 in advance. Hence the virtual maintainer sets the sequence of the τ to service s_2 as #1 and the τ to s_1 as #2 according to the maximum id of r_1. Next, all of the maintenances are pending. The actual maintenances are activated when the related requests arrive at the computational resources, i.e., the requests to the s_1 instances on r_1 and r_2 respectively. The HAND handler in the resources (r_1 and r_2) invokes $\mu_{id}(s_1, r_1)$ to query the current maintaining sequence of requested service (s_1) on responding resources. Naturally, the returned id is greater than the local. The new atomic maintenances then are instantiated in m_1 ($m_1 \rightarrow \tau_2^{r_2}$ and $m_2 \rightarrow \tau_1^{r_1}, \tau_2^{r_1}$

respectively). After executing maintenance of τ_1 and τ_2 on the resources, the actual execution of s_1 is activated. Because there is no request for s_1 on r_1, the maintenance on resource r_3 will never be activated.

In this approach, the actual maintenance is issued when the latest requests arrived at the concrete resources. The maintenance is working in an asynchronous way. Even if the maintenance procedure is broken by an emergent fault, the arriving normal requests will automatically activate the maintenances. Furthermore, it provides a flexible and on-demand maintenance approach. Sequentially, the efficiency of maintenance is promised.

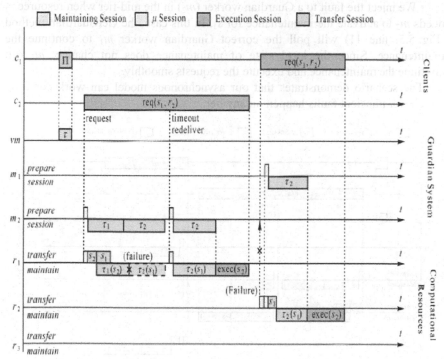

Fig. 5.5. A typical fully asynchronous and failure free maintaining sequence

5.5 Characteristics Discussion

In this section we discuss the fault tolerance capability, archiving mechanism and applicabilities for the applications of our asynchronous model.

5.5.1 Transient Fault Tolerance

As mentioned in Section 5.1, we pursue the tolerating capability for transient failures. We use the same heuristic example in Section 5.4 and inject the transient failures in the end-tier and the mid-tier to demonstrate how our model tolerates faults. As shown in Fig. 5.6.

• We inject the first fault on end-tier (r_1) when executing the τ_2 for service s_1. Because the algorithm in Fig. 5.3 updates the *localId* to the latest finished atomic maintenance (line 14), the later requests (normally requested by time-out strategy in the client-tier) will activate the later task and continue the maintenance. Hence, the asynchronous model can tolerate the transient failures that happened in the end-tier.

• We inject the fault to a Guardian worker (m_2) in the mid-tier when resource r_2 needs m_2 to activate the maintenance for s_1. In this case, the GetGuardian method (Fig. 5.5, line 11) will poll the correct Guardian worker m_1 to continue the maintenance. Since the local state of maintenance does not change, m_1 can continue the maintenance and execute the requests smoothly.

The scenario demonstrates that our asynchronous model can work correctly whichever transient faults happen on any tier.

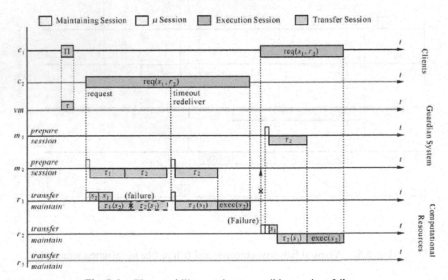

Fig. 5.6.   The capability to tolerate possible transient failures

5.5.2   *Archive Pending Tasks*

One point in the proposed model is critical with respect to the resource consumption: The memory used by the Guardian workers grows linearly with the number of maintaining requests. To address this, we implement an archive mechanism to place the pending tasks into a database or a dumping file (decided by the configuration). If some planned maintenances are not requested for a fixed period, these tasks will be dumped from the Guardian workers memory into a local file or a database record. The fixed period is configured from the admin client. If some new requests that arrive in the end resources are for the archived maintenance, the responding Guardian worker will load it from the archived media and deliver the related atomic maintenance to a target platform. In this way, we can avoid the Guardian system running out of memory over a long period.

5.5.3 *Applicability*

There is definitely no approach that can adapt all the applications in a grid. Our asynchronous model also has shortages for some specific applications.

• We can't promise that each maintenance for heterogeneous resources finishes in a predictable time because the virtual maintainer and Guardian workers are working asynchronously. Hence, if the application demands that the maintenances should finish completely on all related resources before the later tasks, it will benefit little from the asynchronous model.

• The client may wait for a long time if it requests a new service from the resources which accumulated a group of maintenances. In this case, the client tier may need a fault tolerant mechanism to avoid the possible loss from the first access. The feedback mechanism provided by the Guardian (see Chapter 4) can help the client application achieve the maintenance states at runtime.

• The asynchronous model is not appropriate for maintenances on the hardware or the operating system. Because these fundamental upgrades need a rebooting system, the HAND handlers in target resources are forbidden to receive the administrating privileges. In addition, it can't promise that the system can be correctly back online after these operations.

5.6 Correctness Proof

In this section, we show the correctness proof of our implementation described in Section 5.3.1.

Theorem 5.1 (Uniform Agreement) If a Guardian worker in M executes $\tau_p^{r_k}(s_k,op)(1 \le p \le \infty)$, then all correct Guardian workers in M will eventually roll the states to $\tau_p^{r_k}(s_k,op)$.

Proof. By contradiction, suppose that a Guardian worker m_i in M executes $\tau_p^{r_k}(s_k,op)$, and another correct Guardian worker m_j in M executes $\tau_p^{r_k}(s_{k'},op')$ that $s_{k'} \ne s_k$ or $op' \ne op$. From the pseudocode of Fig. 5.3 (lines 11 to 19), it follows that to execute $\tau_p^{r_k}(s_k, op)$, m_i should invoke GetGuard(p, r_k) which returns $\tau_p(s_k, op)$. Meanwhile the return value of GetGuard(p, r_k) invocation for m_j is $\tau_p(s_{k'}, op')$. All the maintenance task is inserted into manstack from Fig. 5.1 (lines 19 to 20), including $\tau_p(s_k, op)$ and $\tau_p(s_{k'}, op')$. Without loss of generality, we suppose that $\tau_p(s_k, op)$ is inserted in manstack by m_i and $\tau_p(s_{k'}, op')$ is inserted in manstack by m_j. Consequently, the p-th maintenance task will be both $\tau_p(s_k, op)$ (invoked by m_i) and $\tau_p(s_{k'}, op')$ (invoked by m_j) while $s_{k'} \neq s_k$ or $op' \neq op$. The value of the p-th maintenance task should be modified between two invocations. However from the line 19 of Fig. 5.1, we know that the sequenced stack is written at most once, i.e., $s_{k'} = s_k$ and $op' = op$. This is a contradiction.

Theorem 5.2 (Uniform Integrity) $\forall r_i \in R$, every Guardian worker in M executes $\tau_p^{r_i}(s_k, op)$ at most once.

Proof. By contradiction, without loss of generality, we suppose that a Guardian worker m_i in M executes $\tau_p(s_k, op)$ twice. Then m_i should invoke GetGuard(p, r_i) operation twice to acquire the maintenance task $\tau_p(s_k, op)$. However, from the line 11 of Fig. 5.3, we know that each time GetGuard(p, r_i) has been invoked, the value of k is incremented to $k+1$. Thus all the sequence numbers should be read only once. Hence GetGuard(p, r_i) operation can't be invoked twice for a single Guardian worker. This is a contradiction.

Theorem 5.3 (Uniform Maintaining Order) If $\prod_{id+k} \cap \prod_{id} = P(k \geq 0)$ and $P \neq \varnothing$, then

(i) $\forall \tau_{id'}^r \in P$ should follow the sequence defined in $\prod_{id}$.

(ii) In particular, $\forall m_i \in M$ can't execute $\tau_{id'+1}^r$ if it has not previously executed $\tau_{id'}$ on the resource r.

Proof.

(i) $\forall \tau_i \in P$, i.e., $\tau_i \in \prod_{id+k} \cap \prod_{id}(k \geq 0)$, so we can see that τ_i is an atomic maintenance that exits both in $\prod_{id}$ and $\prod_{id+k}$. From lines 17 to 23 of the algorithm in Fig. 5.1, once $\prod_{id}$ has been analyzed and pushed into the maintenance stack, the return value of $\mu(s_i, r_i)$ should be null if τ_i has never been pushed into the maintenance stack. Therefore τ_i has been inserted for the first time. According to Definition 5.2, the *id* in $\tau_{id}^r(TS, R, op)$ denotes the global sequence number of the maintenance task. Consequently, $\prod_{id+k}$ will be processed later than $\prod_{id}$. When a virtual maintainer analyzes $\prod_{id+k}$, we can get $\mu(s_i, r_i) \neq$ null since τ_i is already inserted previously by $\prod_{id}$. According to Theorems 5.1 and 5.2, no Guardian worker can access τ_i at the same time. Thus τ_i will not be inserted into the maintenance stack twice. It follows the sequence defined in the operation set $\prod_{id}$ relating to its inserted actions.

(ii) By contradiction, suppose that Guardian worker m_j in M can execute $\tau_{id'+1}$ on r, but has not previously executed $\tau_{id'}$ on the resource r. Without loss of generality, we suppose that the prior maintenance task before the execution of $\tau_{id'+1}$ for m_j on resource r is τ_q and $q \neq id'$. From line 11 of Fig. 5.3, it follows that after m_j executes the function GetGuard(q, r), the global maintainer returns a value as $\tau_q(s_k, op)$. The value of k in the algorithm is equal to q, while $localId = q - 1$ in meantime. Then m_j executes lines 12 to 14, the value of $localId$ is changed to q. No matter statements 15 to 17 will be executed or not, the procedure will turn back to line 10 due to the loop. The value of $localId+1$ is given to k, i.e., $k = q+1$. According to our previous assumption, the maintenance task τ_{q+1} should be returned for the invocation of GetGuard($q+1$, r_i). We understand that GetGuard($q+1$, r_i) would return the ($q+1$)th task in the sequenced operation stack. However, the maintenance task $\tau_{id'+1}$ has an index as $id'+1$. This case will come into existence if and only if $q+1 = id'+1$. It denotes that q should be equal to id' which contradicts our supposition. This is a contradiction.

Accordingly, the proposed algorithms can guarantee uniform maintaining order.
Theorem 5.4 (Correctness of Normal Requests) Once a maintenance task $\prod_{id}(TS, R, OP)$ has been submitted in time t, $\forall s_i \in TS$, any requests to s_i after t should be executed in the states of $\prod_{id}$.

Proof. For $s_i \in TS$, $\exists \tau_{id'}(s_i, r) \in \prod_{id}(r \in R)$ according to the algorithm (lines 2 to 15) in Fig. 5.1. There are two possibilities for $\tau_{id'}$.

Case 1: $\tau_{id'} \notin \bigcup_{k=0}^{id-1} \prod_k$. In this case, according to the algorithm in Fig. 5.3, the action that an atomic maintenance task $\tau_{id'}$ has been executed in time t denotes that the program is rolling to line 13, i.e., $m_p.run(\tau_{id'})$. However, the status of resource s_i is changed to maintenance at time $t - t'(t' > 0)$ before the loop (lines 10 to 18). Thus, all the requests to resource s_i after time $t - t'$ will receive the response of service unavailable. During the execution of task τ_{id} , the resource s_i is always inaccessible till τ_{id} is finished which takes a period of time t'' from the beginning of maintaining task τ_{id} . The states of the resource s_i are already transformed to the states of τ_{id} . The service s_i on resource r will become available in a while (after $t + t''$). Consequently, the requests to resource

s_i after t will either be unavailable or a success in the states of $\prod_{id}$.

Case 2: $\tau_{id'} \in \bigcup_{k=0}^{id-1} \prod_k$. In this case, $\exists q(q > 0), \tau_{id'} \in \prod_q$. According to

Theorem 5.3, $\tau_{id'}$ should follow the sequence defined in $\prod_q$. If the maintenance $\tau_{id'} \in \prod_q$ has been executed correctly before t on the requested resources, then no more maintenances are needed for s_i on those resources. It is equal to the states of execution $\prod_{id}$. Otherwise, if $\tau_{id'} \in \prod_q$ is not executed before, then the situation is the same as case 1.

Eventually, we can ensure that the requests to s_i after t will be executed in the states of $\prod_{id}$.

5.7   Evaluations

In this section, we assess the performance of the existing mechanism and our solution on the test bed of ChinaGrid (see Chapter 2). All the member nodes are connected by the China Education and Research Network (CERNET).

5.7.1   *Environment Settings*

In the experiments, we adopt three heterogeneous clusters mentioned in the following as the target resources. The network bandwidth between those clusters is connected by a 1 Gbps backbone which is shared by other CERNET research applications nationwide.

• *PC Cluster*: A cluster of 16 PCs connected by 100 Mbps Ethernet. Each machine in the cluster has a 1.0 GHz Pentium-III processor, 512 MB RAM. All the nodes are equipped with Red Hat Linux with kernel 2.4.20-8.

• *Hybrid Cluster*: An IBM p630 server with dual Power4 1.0 GHz processors, 4 GB RAM. Suse Linux with kernel 2.6.18-34 is deployed on the server; Two Dawning nodes have dual AMD Opteron 242 1.6 GHz processors, 2 GB RAM. All the servers are connected by 100 Mbps Ethernet.

• *High Performance Computing Cluster*: A cluster of 36 servers are connected by 1 Gbps Ethernet. Each node has 64 bit quad 2.0 GHz Xeon processors, 4 GB RAM. The operating system deployed on these resources is Red Hat Enterprise Linux Application Server v4 with kernel version 2.6.18.

The JVMs used in the experiment environment are 1.5.0_06-b05 mixed mode implemented by SUN for x86 servers, and 1.5.0-b2.3 ppc-64 implemented by IBM for PowerPC servers respectively.

5.7.2 Metrics

In the experiments, three main metrics are adopted to identify the improvements.

• *Maintaining Duration* denotes the duration from the start of maintenance to the time when the first related resource is available.

• *Saved Server Time* (SST) represents the sum of the saved time for each related resource. The saved time here means the duration between the available time of the specific resource (t_r) and the completed time for all related maintenances (t_{man}).

$$SST = \sum_{r \in R}(t_{man} - t_r) \qquad (5.1)$$

• *Improved Rate* (IR) depicts the improved utilization of a specific maintaining approach against the total maintaining time for all related resources in the synchronous mode. The R are related resources defined in $\prod$.

$$IR = \frac{SST}{t_{man} \cdot \|R\|} \qquad (5.2)$$

5.7.3 Applications

We take an Image Processing Service (Zhou *et al.*, 2005) deployed in ChinaGrid (Wu *et al.*, 2005) as our test case. The related service packages and their relationships are listed in Table 5.1. The application client needs to employ many service instances to finish the related image processing. In our experiment, all of the staging data are stored in the local system temporally to save the experimenting time. The composed image processing service is dependent on a logging service, transferring service and general running service respectively. That means there are, at most, 6 implicatational maintenances for maintaining this service to the target platform.

Table 5.1 Maintaining operations

Main task	Description	Operation	Pack. size (MB)
τ_1	General Running Service v1.0	*deploy*	1.4
τ_2	Transfer Service v1.0	*deploy*	6.5
τ_3	Logging Service v1.2	*patch*	4.1
τ_4	Logging Service v1.3	*patch*	4.1
τ_5	Image Processing Service v1.0	*deploy*	18.0
τ_6	Image Processing Service v1.1	*patch*	5.2

5.7.4   Overheads

Because our solution needs to deploy the HAND handler to the target resources, we evaluated the overhead brought by HAND for the normal requests in this section. We drove a client accessing the Image Processing Service and Logging Service 1,000 times from the remote sites to the service instances deployed on the heterogenous resources separately. For the convenience of comparison, we also assessed the response time for normal requests without the HAND handler. Table 5.2 depicts the results. It is clear that the cost of HAND handler varies from 29.09 ms to 82.30 ms for the image processing service and 41.47 ms to 79.06 ms for the logging service respectively in different systems. Although the cost for the short-term running jobs is high, it is acceptable for long-term running tasks which are widely seen in grid applications.

Table 5.2   The overhead on the end-tier with 95% confidence

	P3($\pm\Delta$, ms)	Ppc($\pm\Delta$, ms)	Opteron($\pm\Delta$, ms)	Xeon($\pm\Delta$, ms)
1	210.80±4.75	178.50±6.26	162.74±4.06	147.74±1.70
2	131.74±1.34	125.22±1.40	111.26±1.92	106.27±1.56
3	393.35±7.07	331.92±4.43	306.59±5.48	190.24±3.52
4	311.05±1.89	275.04±2.97	236.10±1.74	161.15±7.08

1. logging service; 2. logging service (normal); 3. image processing service; 4. image processing service (normal)

Besides the cost to the response to normal requests, we also evaluated the maintaining duration (i.e., service unavailable period) for different physical platforms. Table 5.3 lists the time cost for deploying the image processing service. All the costs were measured for the atomic maintenances. The results show that the Weakest Link Effect in the grids is serious. To deploy it in a clean environment (not including the diversity of network bandwidth), we cost about 68.1 s for the PIII system, 49.5 s for the IBM p630 system, 33.2 s for the Opteron system and 17.0 s for the quad Xeon system. The longest duration is near to quadruple the shortest.

Table 5.3   The maintaining duration for heterogeneous machines with 95% confidence

	P3($\pm\Delta$, ms)	Ppc($\pm\Delta$, ms)	Opteron($\pm\Delta$, ms)	Xeon($\pm\Delta$, ms)
τ_1	10,632.93±150.54	7,885.70±145.55	5,061.00±141.40	2,552.19±71.39
τ_2	10,186.07±133.62	7,549.20±121.16	4,766.40±137.76	2,491.70±80.91
τ_3	14,519.79±248.96	10,244.93±118.39	7,411.63±237.23	4,131.20±116.17
τ_4	9,988.38±133.71	7,298.33±181.51	4,207.77±111.40	2,249.81±76.78
τ_5	12,759.90±289.09	8.991.13±160.22	7,180.60±372.56	3,090.50±124.67
τ_6	10,013.10±138.40	7,551.17±151.68	4,612.83±130.84	2,453.95±68.69

5.7.5   Evaluations in Cluster and Grid

In this section, we repeated the experiments on the HPC cluster and a hybrid grid environment (including all of the clusters mentioned above). To demonstrate the effectiveness and efficiency, we decoupled the hidden tasks into atomic maintenances (varying from τ_1 to τ_6 in the vertical) to the target resources (varying from 1 node to 32 nodes in the horizontal). Fig. 5.7 depicts the maintaining duration separately. From Fig. 5.7, we can find that the improvement by using our asynchronous maintenance in the homogeneous cluster environment against the traditional synchronous approach is limited. Even in the peak point (τ_6, 32 nodes), the improvement is about 18.9 s. With the growth of nodes and maintaining tasks, the improvement is not much either. However, the maintaining duration for the grid (as shown in Fig. 5.7) is definitely greater than that for the homogeneous cluster. Because the total maintaining time increases due to the network diversities, the total maintaining time is up to 2,889.0 s. In that period, we can guarantee 2,855.3 s of available time for the global system by adopting our asynchronous model. This proves that the asynchronous model effectively reduces the Weakest Link Effect. To understand the characteristics of our asynchronous approach clearly, we zoom in on the asynchronous part in Fig. 5.7. From that, we can find that the duration does not grow with the varying of the node scale. The reason is that the system can be available when the quickest maintenance is finished. Accordingly, our model can guarantee the shortest downtime for a distributed system.

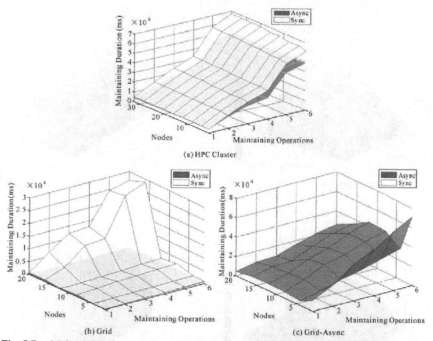

Fig. 5.7. Maintaining duration for grid and cluster in different scales of nodes and operations

Other than the duration, we also conducted the measure of SST and IR both in the two environments. The metric SST helps us understand how much time our solution can save for the maintenance in a distributed environment. In addition, the metric IR expresses the ratio of available serving time against the whole maintaining duration. Fig. 5.8 demonstrates the results. Comparing Fig. 5.8(a) with Fig. 5.8(c), we can find that the saved maintaining time will be accumulative, as much as the growth in nodes scale and complexity of maintenance. In particular, it achieves uneven improvement in the heterogeneous grid. And the saved cost exceeds 48,416.0 s in the peak point (20 nodes, τ_6) for the grid. In the homogeneous HPC cluster, this trend is continuous and the value is relatively less (less than about 100 times). Fig. 5.8(b) and Fig. 5.8(d) show that our approach can achieve an available time increase of 27.0% at most in the HPC cluster and 91.7% in the grid environments. Another interesting phenomenon in Fig. 5.8(b) and Fig. 5.8(d) is that the value of IR is affected by the complexity of maintenance more than the node scale in the homogeneous cluster but it is the contrary in the grid. The reason is that the asynchronous maintenance improves the IR mainly by saving the transfer time of separate maintaining packages. Hence, with the maintaining operation increasing, the improvement in IR changes much. However, the heterogeneity of different nodes is more important in the grid environment. It is decided by the weakest link of the target resource. These results prove that our solution can overcome the Weakest Link Effect efficiently and effectively.

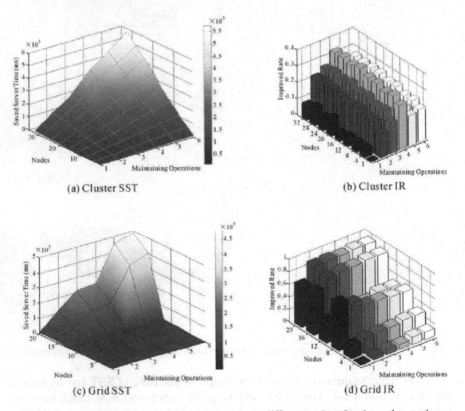

(a) Cluster SST

(b) Cluster IR

(c) Grid SST

(d) Grid IR

Fig. 5.8. Maintaining duration for grid and cluster in different scales of nodes and operations

5.8   Summary

In this chapter we present an asynchronous maintaining model in our Guardian system for heterogenous grid services. To effectively reduce the *Weakest Link Effect* caused by *heterogeneity* and *transient failures* of maintenance, our model uses a three-tier asynchronous architecture to represent how the tiers promise the time sequence and improve the efficiency and availability of global grid systems. The contributions of our solution mainly include:

(i) It is general enough to apply to grid applications without modifying upper business logic;

(ii) With minor costs for processing a normal request, it can provide high efficiency and availability for a distributed computing system. In particular, it is adaptable for the heterogeneous grid and tolerant of emergent faults.

(iii) It can detect the implicational maintenances among heterogeneous resources and quickly propagate complicated maintenance instructions or provisioning to the large-scale nodes safely.

References

Foster I, Kesselman C (1998) The Grid: Blueprint for a New Computing Infrastructure. Morgan Kaufmann Publishers, San Francisco, USA, pp. 3-12.

Gross JL, Tucker TW (2001) Topological Graph Theory. Courier Dover.

Jin H (2004) Chinagrid: Making grid computing a reality. In: Chen Z, Chen H, Miao Q, Fu Y, Fox E, Lim E (eds.) Digital Libraries: International Collaboration and Cross-Fertilization. Springer, Singapore, pp. 13-24.

Jin H, Qi L, Wu S, Luo Y, Dai J (2007) Dependency-aware maintenance for dynamic grid services. In: Li J, Zhang X (eds.) The 39th International Conference on Parallel Processing, 2007. IEEE Computer Society, Xi'an, China, pp. 64-71.

Qi L, Jin H, Foster I, Gawor J (2007a) Hand: Highly available dynamic deployment infrastructure for globus toolkit 4. In: Vecchia GD, di Serafino D, Marra I, Perla F (eds.) 15th Euromicro International Conference on Parallel, Distributed and Network-Based Processing (PDP 2007). IEEE Computer Society, Naples, Italy, pp. 155-162.

Qi L, Jin H, Luo Y, Shi X, Wang C (2007b) Service dependency model for dynamic and stateful grid services. In: Jin H (ed.) The 7th International Conference on Algorithms and Architetures for Parallel Processing. Springer Verlag, Hangzhou, China, pp. 278-289.

Sabharwal R (2006) Grid infrastructure deployment using smartfrog technology. In: Bader DA, Khokhar AA (eds.) International Conference on Networking and Services. 2006. IEEE Computer Society, Washington, DC, USA, p. 73.

Salemie G (2006) The weakest link: The impact of wide area networking on networked application performance. In: the 2006 ACM/IEEE Conference on Supercomputing. ACM, Tampa, Florida, USA, pp. 288-292.

Shankar CS, Talwar V, Iyer S, Chen Y, Milojicic DS, Campbell RH (2006) Specification-enhanced policies for automated management of changes in IT systems. In: LeFebvre W(ed.) The 20th Conference on Systems Administration (LISA 2006). USENIX Association, Washington, DC, USA, pp. 103-118.

Shwartz L, Ayachitula N, Maheswaran S, Grabarnik G (2005) Managing system capabilities and requirements using rough set theory. Research Report RC23699, IBM.

Talwar V, Milojicic D, Wu Q (2005) Approaches for service deployment. IEEE Internet Computing, 9(2): 70-80.

Wu Y, Wu S, Yu H, Hu C (2005) Cgsp: An extensible and reconfigurable grid framework. In: Yang LT (ed.) The 6th International Workshop on Advanced Parallel Processing Technologies. Springer, Hong Kong, China, pp. 292-300.

Zhou H, Yang X, Liu H, Tang Y (2005) First evaluation of parallel methods of automatic global image registration based on wavelets. In: Jose D, Feng W (eds.) International Conference on Parallel Processing, 2005. IEEE Computer Society, Oslo, Norway, pp. 129-136.

Zielinski K, Jarzab M, Kosinski J (2005) Role of n1 technology in the next generation grids middleware. In: Sloot PM, Hoekstra AG, Priol T, Reinefeld A, Bubak M (eds.) Advances in Grid Computing—EGC 2005. Springer, Amsterdam, The Netherlands, pp. 942-951.

6

Orchestrating Provisioning among Heterogeneous Middleware

Abstract: After several years of development, the computational infrastructure has been widely developed. In particular, when the grid technology grows to production level, users have several options to handle resourceless problems when submitting large-scale jobs to the infrastructure. The capability of dynamic provisioning, fast deployment of virtual machines and interoperation can help users complete their jobs correctly even if the local resources are not adequate. To orchestrate these approaches well and find the optimal solution for end users, this chapter proposes a novel orchestrating model to optimize these approaches efficiently. An image processing application running on three heterogeneous grid platforms is adopted to demonstrate the efficiency and capability of the proposed model. The result proved that the optimal solution can efficiently orchestrate the jobs among the grids.

6.1 Introduction

As we discussed in Chapter 2, Open Grid Services Architecture (OGSA), proposed by Open Grid Forum (OGF), is dedicated to defining the behavior of grid middleware at a standard level. After ten years' development, there are a group of production grid platforms, such as Globus Toolkit (Foster, 2006), gLite (Munro *et al.*, 2006), SUN Grid Engine (Gentzsch, 2001), Unicore (Erwin, 2002), ChinaGrid Support Platform (Wu *et al.*, 2005) and so forth. Despite all of these implementations claiming that they are following OGSA specifications, few of them are interoperable due to the heterogeneous nature of different implementations. Because of this limitation, end users in different virtual organizations still have to face the resourceless problem when massive users access the infrastructure at the same time. The resourceless concept discussed in this chapter means that when domain users submit their jobs to the computation infrastructure, there are not adequate resources for allocation due to the limits and unavailability of the working environment. Thus, users have to wait until the resources are available for scheduling.

To resolve the resourceless problem, we have several possible opinions. First, by introducing the interoperability of grid systems, users can access the alien virtual organization resources with different platforms even if the local organization can't provide available resources. Second, users can use the dynamical provisioning (deploying) capability to expand the available resources. Finally, another important technology, the virtual machine, can help domain users resolve the resourceless challenge. The contribution is to use the virtual workspace service proposed by Globus alliance. By invoking the responding service, domain users can freely provided their working spaces to the target virtual machines and finish their requests dynamically.

We demonstrate the resourceless problem by a use case in Fig. 6.1. As shown in Fig. 6.1(a), when the domain user submits a job with demands of 12+ nodes, the transferring cost should be below 20 GB. However, there are only five available resources in the local grid (marked as Heterogeneous Grid 1). Definitely, without adequate resources, the submitted job can't be activated. As mentioned in the comments, the user can make three approaches to match the executing requirements (as marked in Fig. 6.1(a)):

• The resources can be leased from other grid middleware. The dashed box 1 contained seven resources from two alien grids respectively.

• The requested services can be dynamically deployed to the available nodes. The dashed box 2 contained seven resources from the local grid whose statuses are ready but not available for execution.

• The requested services can be dynamically deployed within a virtual machine template to clean nodes. The dashed box 3 contained seven resources from newly added nodes which are totally clean even without the operating system. The images will contain all necessary workspace, the grid container and support library.

However, high efficiency and availability are always the major objective pursued by the middleware in heterogeneous grids. We address this problem and are dedicated to finding optimal solutions for end users to achieve high efficiency and least cost (e.g. IO cost).

How to adopt an adaptive approach to finish the job requests in the meantime and achieve the highest efficiency both in the terms of the end user and the grid resources is becoming a new challenge when we face the options of choosing interoperation, virtual workspace and dynamic provisioning. In this chapter, our idea is to explicitly predicate the cost of jobs before the submission and decide the specific approach according to the runtime statuses of grid systems.

The proposed mechanism and its implementation have the following contributions: (i) By adaptively adopting the dynamic provisioning (including the application packages and the OS images) and the heterogeneous submission, we can achieve high efficiency for end users; (ii) Utilizations of servers in different grids can be much enhanced; (iii) Users can access the alien grids by using the same interface without scarifying any features of the domain distributed applications.

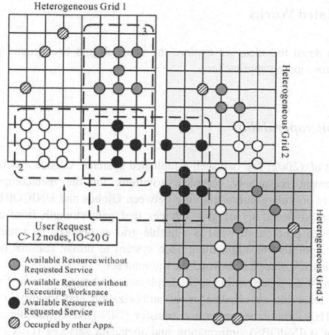

(a) Computing resources in isolated grids

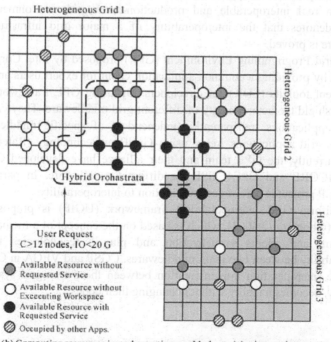

(b) Computing resources in orchestration-enabled provisioning environment

Fig. 6.1. Three approaches for adoption

6.2   Related Works

Before we detail the idea, we explore the research and background relating to different provisioning approaches.

6.2.1   Interoperability

Snelling *et al.* (2002) use two well-established systems, Globus and UNICORE, that implement reasonably complete solutions for the metacomputing grid problem. By providing interoperability between Globus and UNICORE, this will result in an advanced set of grid services that gain strength from each other, addressing the problem of what is a usable grid as opposed to a minimal grid. GRIP gains pointers to augmenting each system to utilize features not initially contained in each other, i.e., beyond the minimal set.

The GIN-CG group within OGF implements interoperation in five specific areas. By resolving the challenges of authorization and identity management (GIN-AUTH), data management and transfer (GIN-DATA), job description and submission (GIN-JOBS), information and metadata services (GIN-INFO), and operations experience of applications (GIN-OPS), the GIN project is dedicated to building a real interoperable and production-level grid environment. Recent progress denotes that the interoperability of a major grid infrastructure and middleware is proved.

The Grid Programming Environment (GPE) proposed by Intel Corporation is motivated by providing a common application client for expert users and a suit of development toolkits (SDK) for developers. By using GPE framework, domain users can shield the heterogeneity of different grid middleware. They can develop the grid applications transparently (independent of specific middleware) and access the grid applications freely using GridBean technology (Ratering *et al.*, 2006). Currently, the GPE team and their alliance have developed GPE4GTK, GPE4UNICORE and GPE4CGSP for different middleware. In particular, the GPE4CGSP project is part of our contribution to interoperability.

A Uniform Grid Interoperability Framework (UGIF) is proposed in the literature (Gong *et al.*, 2003), which is based on the concept of a mediated bridge mechanism, and adopts virtualization and plug-in technologies to achieve interoperability between two main middlewares, CGSP and VEGA in China. With UGIF, the interoperation implementation between these two grid systems, as a case study, becomes a reality without changing their codes.

6.2.2 Dynamic Provisioning

The virtual workspace service, proposed by Globus Alliance (Keahey *et al.*, 2005), introduces the concept of a configurable execution environment that can be created and managed as a first-class entity to reflect client requirements. Such workspaces can be dynamically deployed on a variety of resources decoupling the notion of environment and resource.

As discussed in Chapters 3 and 4, HAND (Qi *et al.*, 2007) and Guardian (Jin *et al.*, 2007), are motivated by providing a dynamic deployment of inter-dependent grid services without shutting down the hosting system and scarifying the availability and the efficiency of the global system. The Guardian system can adapt users' demands during the runtime by introducing several granularities of deployment.

Other similar efforts (Hailong *et al.*, 2006; Smith *et al.*, 2004; Weissman *et al.*, 2005) also address the capability of dynamic provisioning for the grid system.

6.2.3 Scheduling in a Distributed System

In the age of cluster computing, multiprocessor tasks scheduling became a hot topic. Investigations developed a series of algorithms to find optimal solutions for scheduling on multiprocessors. Parallel applications are often represented as DAGs. The DAGs are highly data-dependent and can be precisely known after the execution rather than before. In the literature (Drozdowski, 1996), the jobs distinguish three types of dedicated processor systems: flow-shop, open-shop and job-shop. In the flow-shop, all tasks have the same number of operations which are performed sequentially and require the same sets of processors. In the open-shop, the order among the operations is immaterial. For the job-shop, the sequence of operations and the sets of required processors are defined for each task separately. However, most scheduling problems are NP-hard problems. It is not acceptable when we demand fast decisions that are made before submission.

Maculan *et al.* (1999) considered the problem of scheduling dependent tasks onto heterogeneous multiprocessor architecture, but neglected communication time. Davidovi' *et al.* (2007) considered the multiprocessor scheduling problem with communication delays, where the delay is proportional to both the amount of exchanged data between pairs of dependent tasks and the distance between processors in the multiprocessor architecture. However, even after optimization and reducing variables, the time complexity of the algorithm is still $O(n^2 \cdot m)$. Even after optimization it is hard to get an ideal solution in an acceptable time from the client side.

6.3   Orchestrating Model

In this section we will introduce related concepts and the problem formulation.

6.3.1   *Definitions*

Definition 6.1 (Heterogeneous Grid Platforms) The heterogeneous grid defined here means the computational infrastructures that are equipped with different middleware software (marked as G). Normally, the grid middleware follows the OGSA standards and includes the functionality of deploying, registering, discovering, running and monitoring the grid infrastructure and applications. For instance, each middleware should be implemented under the common specification of Web services. The representations include Globus Toolkit 4.0 (Foster, 2006), UNICORE (Erwin, 2002), VEGA (Gong *et al.*, 2003) and CGSP (Jin, 2004) discussed in Chapter 2.

Definition 6.2 (Grid Job) Grid job (marked as J) is the job submitted by domain users to the grid platforms. The grid jobs can be composed in a workflow or job arrays.

Definition 6.3 (Grid Resources and Lifecycle) Grid resources (marked as R) are the computing and storage computing resources deployed in the IT infrastructure which can be leased for the expert domains computation. Examples include the various computational machines, instruments, storage equipment and so on. In this chapter, we adopt the resources which support the management interface for Web services. As the properties of the grid resources, the static metrics such as CPU frequency, memory, storage capability and so on are important for provisioning applications in runtime. The dynamic metrics definitely include the utilization of the CPU, free memory, available storage capability and so on, which are rather important for dynamically choosing resources (i.e., job scheduling). As shown in Fig. 6.2, we classify the resource types into four states of the lifecycle according to the requested services and runtime situations.

• Resources which have not deployed any software and even operating systems (marked as s_1).

• Resources which have not deployed related services but have been deployed into some specific grid platforms (marked as s_2).

• Resources which have deployed related services (marked as s_3) and they are available for accepting user's requests (marked as s_3).

• Resources which have been leased by some other application. Namely, they are unavailable for current request (marked as s_4).

Each of these states can be changed to the other states once the (un)leasing, VM (de)provisioning or (un)deploying operations have happened. Normally, these maintaining operations are provided by each grid middleware separately.

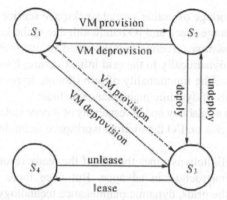

Fig. 6.2. Resource status transitions

Definition 6.4 (Resourceless Phenomenon) Resourceless defined in this chapter means that the grid infrastructure can't provide adequate available resources to process the jobs when no further maintenances or interoperations are issued. In particular, we assume that there are the following resource limits in heterogeneous grid middlewares (g).

• $L = \{l_1, l_2, ..., l_g\}$ is the limit-collection of available resources with targeted services (in state s_3);

• $M = \{m_1, m_2, ..., m_g\}$ is the limit-collection of available resources without targeted services but has deployed basic middleware (in state s_2);

• $N = \{n_1, n_2, ..., n_g\}$ is the number of available resources without targeted services and even without the supported operating system (in state s_1).

Normally, if the number of demanded resources is greater than l_g in a specific grid middleware g, we define this by saying that users meet the resourceless phenomenon.

6.3.2 Optional Solutions for Resourceless Execution

As mentioned in Section 6.1, three approaches are discussed to help resolve the resourceless problem. In this section, the pros and cons of different approaches are demonstrated as follows.

• *Virtual Workspace Technology* proposed by Globus Alliance is designed to deploy the virtual machine images dynamically to target resources on demand. In this way, all the service and staging data can be constrained in a single virtual machine. The benefits of the virtual technologies include:

- It provides high capability of service isolation for computing. The reason is that all of the execution information is encapsulated in the stand-alone virtual machines.

- It is easy for maintenances. Within the virtual machines, an administrator only needs to construct or destroy the working space in a common template image file and then can directly deploy this to the target resources.

However, the shortage of usable virtual workspace service means that the user would cost much storage space and IO bandwidth due to the large image files.

• *Dynamic Maintenance Technology* proposed in our previous chapters is to deploy applications dynamically to the grid infrastructure. Using this solution, end users can also achieve the functionality of provisioning to resolve the resourceless problem. The benefits of dynamic maintenance include:

- It provides good availability and the capability of service isolation to some extent.

- There is minor cost on I/O than virtual workspace technology in the distributed systems.

This solution definitely assumes that all of the ready resources have equipped the deployment infrastructure in advance. But once there are new and clean resources joined to the grids, dynamic maintenance technology can benefit little in resolving the problem.

• *Interoperability Approaches.* The efforts (Open Grid Forum, 2005) of different grid platforms can help us access the optional alien computing or storage resources in various grid platforms. Its benefits are as follows:

- Neither operating system nor applications are necessarily deployed before executing the jobs in advance. Thus, end users can start the job in the meantime without any provisioning actions.

- In this approach, the utilization and availability of back-end resources can be improved.

However, running the jobs among the alien middleware should take into consideration the cost of heterogeneity, security and the different nature of the various middleware. These factors will also cost much more total execution time.

6.3.3 *Classic Formulation*

Scheduling the multi-tasks among processors is widely discussed in the distributed area. 0-1 programming is a classic model for optimizing the scheduling. We formulate the resourceless problem where the task precedence is modeled by a directed acyclic graph $G = (V, A)$, where V is a set of tasks and an edge (i, j) exists if task i has to be completed before task j. If i and j are executed on different computing resources $h, k \in P$, they incur a communication cost γ_{ij}^{hk} dependent on the distance d_{hk} between the distributed resources, and on the amount of exchanged data c_{ij} between tasks ($\gamma_{ij}^{hk} = \Gamma c_{ij} d_{hk}$, where Γ is a known constant). Here are some symbols for the model. Let $\delta^- \{j\}$ be the set of precedents of task i, that is $\delta^- \{j\} = \{i \in V \mid (i, j) \in A\}$. We have $(\forall i, s \in V, k \in P, g \in G)$, then:

$$y_{ikg}^s = \begin{cases} 1, & \text{task } i \text{ is the } s\text{-th task on processor } k \\ 0, & \text{otherwise} \end{cases} \tag{6.1}$$

We pursue the minimization of makespan C_{max} subject to constraints Eqs. (6.2) to (6.11).

$$\min C_{max}$$

$$
s.t \begin{cases}
\forall i \in V, \sum_{g=1}^{q} \sum_{k=1}^{l_g} \sum_{s=1}^{n} y_{ikg}^s = 1 & (6.2) \\[2mm]
\forall g \in G, k \in P(g), s \in V, \sum_{i=1}^{n} y_{ikg}^s \le 1 & (6.3) \\[2mm]
\forall g \in G, k \in P(g), s \in V - \{1\}, \sum_{i=1}^{n} y_{ikg}^s \le \sum_{i=1}^{n} y_{ikg}^{s+1} & (6.4) \\[2mm]
\forall j \in V, i \in \delta^-\{j\}, t_j \ge t_i + \varepsilon_g \cdot L_i + \sum_{f=1}^{q}\sum_{h=1}^{l_f}\sum_{s=1}^{n}\sum_{g=1}^{q}\sum_{k=1}^{l_g}\sum_{r=1}^{n} \gamma_{ij}^{hk} y_{ihf}^s y_{jkg}^r & \\[2mm]
\qquad\qquad + \sum_{g=1}^{q}\sum_{k=1}^{l_g}\sum_{s=1}^{n}(p_{jkg}^v + p_{jkg}^d) y_{jkg}^s & (6.5) \\[2mm]
\forall g \in G, k \in P(g), s \in V - \{n\}, i,j \in V, t_j \ge t_i + L_i - \alpha[2 - (y_{ikg}^s + \sum_{r=s+1}^{n} y_{jkg}^r)] & (6.6) \\[2mm]
\forall g \in G, \sum_{k=1}^{l_g}\sum_{s=1}^{n}\sum_{i=1}^{n} y_{ikg}^s \le l_g + m_g + n_g & (6.7) \\[2mm]
\forall g \in G, \sum_{k=1}^{l_g}\sum_{s=1}^{n}\sum_{i=1}^{n} p_i^v y_{ikg}^s \le m_g & (6.8) \\[2mm]
\forall g \in G, \sum_{k=1}^{l_g}\sum_{s=1}^{n}\sum_{i=1}^{n} p_i^d y_{ikg}^s \le n_g & (6.9) \\[2mm]
\forall i,s \in V, g \in G, k \in P(g), y_{ikg}^s \in \{0,1\} & (6.10) \\[2mm]
\forall i \in V, t_i \ge 0 & (6.11)
\end{cases}
$$

Here $\alpha \gg 0$ is a sufficiently large penalty coefficient and γ_{ij}^{hk} represent the data staging delay between tasks i and j as mentioned in the previous sections. Eq. (6.2) defines that each task is assigned to exactly one resource. Eq. (6.3) denotes that one task will at least once be the s-th task at resource k, while Formula (6.4) ensures that if some task is the s-th one ($s \le 2$) scheduled to resource k then there must be another task assigned as $(s-1)$-th to the same resource. Eq. (6.5) expresses precedence constraints together with the communication time required for tasks assigned to different processors. Eq. (6.6) means that the sequence of j must start at least L_i time slots after the beginning of task i whenever j is executed after i on the same processor k; the M parameter must be large enough so that Eq. (6.6) is active only if i and j are executed on the same processor k and $r > s$. Eq. (6.7) depicts that all tasks should be executed on the limited resources. The classic model can formulate the problem clearly. However, in this way, the scheduling system suffers in real implementations.

- First, the complexity of this programming problem will be $O(|V|^4 |\bigcup_{g \in G} P_g|^2)$.

By solving the formulation with a Branch-and-Bound method, we need to solve a linear relaxation at each node. It is impossible to find an optimized orchestration solution in acceptable time.

- Second, due to the nature of autonomy, the heterogeneous scheduling modules or services will not permit alien grid middleware to access internal resources. Thus users can't actually orchestrate these resources under this model.

- Third, many parameters such as γ_{ij}^{hk} are hard to predict at runtime.

6.4   Problem Formulation for Resourceless Orchestration

The 0-1 model is relatively complicated when applied in our cases. Thus, we take the integer planning model to simplify it in this chapter. The characteristics and formal formulation of these approaches are depicted in Table 6.1.

Table 6.1   The required parameters for orchestrating the provisioning and interoperations

Phases	Symbol	Explanation	Source
Provisioning (Dynamic maintenance)	$\tilde{d}_s, s \in S$	The size of related deploying service packages S	*Fetch from records of provisioning center*
	$\tilde{b}_{ij}$	The networking bandwidth between provisioning agent i and target resource j	*Fetch from monitoring system*
	$\tilde{t}_{rs}$	The actual deployment time for provisioning service s on resource r	*Fetch from historical statistics*
Provisioning (Virtual workspace)	$\hat{d}_s$	The size of operating system images related to service s	*Fetch from provisioning center*
	$\hat{b}_{ij}$	The bandwidth between the provisioning center and the target resources	*Fetch from the monitoring system*
	$\hat{t}_r$	The actual time to activate the operating system in virtual machine r.	*Fetch from historical statistics*
Execution	$d_{r'r}^{inp}$ $d_{rr''}^{outp}$	The size of resource r's staging data (i.e., Input and output), r' and r'' are the precedence and subsequence of r respectively	*Unpredictable, different to applications*
	$b_{i,j}$	The bandwidth between staging resource i and j	*Fetch from monitoring system*
	ε_g	The slowdown factor for heterogeneous platform g	*Fetch from historic statistics*
	$j(r)$	The execution time for job j running on specific resource r	*Unpredictable, fetch from historical statistics*
	i^{ij}	The factor to reflect the staging-out data from resource i to j. $$i^{ij} = \begin{cases} 0, & d_{ij}^{outp} = d_{ij}^{inp} \\ 1, & \text{else} \end{cases}$$	*Fetch from submitted job*

$$t_d^{prov} = \sum_{s \in S} \max_{g \in G} \max_{r \in R_g} (\frac{\overline{d}_s}{b_{0r}} + \widetilde{t}_{rs})$$ (6.12)

$$t_v^{prov} = \max_{r \in R} (\frac{\hat{d}_s}{b_{0r}} + \hat{t}_r)$$ (6.13)

$$t_n^{exec} = \sum_{j \in J} \max_{g \in G} \max_{r \in R_g} \varepsilon_g \cdot (\frac{d_{r'r}^{inp}}{b_{r'r}} + i^{rr''} \cdot \frac{d_{rr''}^{outp}}{b_{rr''}} + t_{j(r)}^{exec})$$ (6.14)

6.4.1 Constraints for Provisioning

To effectively adopt these solutions for users' computation tasks, we also need to define some constraints for selecting resources. These constraints are based on the demands of end users or global systems.

Constraint 1 (Availability) As discussed in the earlier chapters, the server-side always gives much consideration to global availability. To achieve this, we should issue the minimum deployment time for target resources. Thus, the constraint for target platforms is depicted in Eq. (6.15).

$$A = \frac{t^{exec}}{t_d^{prov} + t_v^{prov} + t^{exec}}$$ (6.15)

Constraint 2 (IO Cost) Since the bandwidth between different resources and grid platforms would vary in cost due to the different accounting strategies that are defined in various grid platforms, we define the total IO cost among grid resources as shown in Eq. (6.16). This mainly includes the cost of transferring operating system images and staging in (out) data for dependent services.

$$C = \sum_{s \in S} \sum_{r \in R} (\widetilde{d}_s + \hat{d}_s) + \sum_{j \in J} \sum_{r \in R} (d_{r'r}^{inp} + i^{rr''} d_{rr''}^{outp})$$ (6.16)

Constraint 3 (Computing Power) The constraints of computing power are mainly set as the baseline for execution of grid jobs. These constraints are considered relative to the complexity of specific domains. We define the constraints in Eq. (6.17).

$$P = \|R\|$$ (6.17)

The constraints are based on the correct execution of a grid application from both user and service-provider viewpoints.

6.4.2   Optimization Goal

We pursue the minimized execution time in a resourceless environment. From Table 6.1 and constraints defined in section 6.4.1, the problem is defined in v (6.18). From Eqs. (6.21) to (6.24), we can conclude that the orchestration between interoperation and provisioning is a non-linear integer programming problem.

$$\min\{t_v^{prov} + t_d^{prov} + t^{exec}\}$$

$$s.t.\begin{cases} \mathscr{A} \geq \ddot{a} & (6.18) \\ \mathscr{C} \leq \ddot{c} & (6.19) \\ \mathscr{H} \leq \ddot{h} & (6.20) \\ \sum_{g \in \mathscr{G}} (x_g + x_g' + x_g'') = \ddot{p} & (6.21) \\ \forall g \in \mathscr{G}, 0 \leq x_g \leq l_g & (6.22) \\ \forall g \in \mathscr{G}, 0 \leq x_g' \leq m_g & (6.23) \\ \forall g \in \mathscr{G}, 0 \leq x_g'' \leq n_g & (6.24) \end{cases}$$

6.5   Implementation of Orchestrator

We implement the orchestrator on the client side. Thus, the domain users can estimate how many resources on earth could be available for leasing during submission of the job. In this way, users can always get an optimal solution for executing their jobs. Fig. 6.3 describes the orchestration algorithm.

6.6   Evaluations

In this section, we use our implementation of Image Processing GridBean to test the capability and orchestrating price respectively. We run the experiments on ChinaGrid test bed.

```
input  : 𝒥 :job collection submitted by users,normally encapsulated in the format of
         JSDL from GridBeans, each jᵢ ∈ J is a parallel division;
         ℛ:The registration of local grid system;
         ρ: Requested resource number;
         ϑ: specific availability;
output: Orchestrating Solution
```

1 foreach $j_i \in \mathscr{J}$ do
2     $(\mathscr{L}, \mathscr{M}, \mathscr{N}) = \mathscr{R}.\texttt{getAvailableBounds}(\mathscr{J})$;
    // set available bounds for different states.
3   foreach $g_k \in \mathscr{G}$ do
4   Object.setConstraint $(\zeta_{s_1 g_k} \leq l_{g_k})$;// $l_{g_k} \in \mathscr{L}$
5   Object.setConstraint $(\zeta_{s_2 g_k} \leq m_{g_k})$;// $m_{g_k} \in \mathscr{M}$
6   Object.setConstraint $(\zeta_{s_3 g_k} \leq n_{g_k})$;// $n_{g_k} \in \mathscr{N}$
7   end
    // set target numbers.
8   Object.setConstraint $(\sum_{g_k \in \mathscr{G}} \zeta_{s_1 g_k} + \zeta_{s_2 g_k} + \zeta_{s_3 g_k} \leq \rho)$;
    // calculate the io cost
9     $\mathscr{S} \leftarrow \mathscr{R}.\texttt{getServices}(j_i)$;
10     $\mathscr{V} \leftarrow \mathscr{R}.\texttt{getVMachine}(j_i)$;
    // Get related virtual machines from virtual workspace
    repository.
11     $d_{prov} \leftarrow \sum_{g_k \in \mathscr{G}} [\zeta_{s_1 g_k} \cdot size(v_{j_i}) + \sum_{p \in \mathscr{S}} \zeta_{s_2 g_k} \cdot size(p)]$;
12     $d_{staging} \leftarrow \sum_{u=1}^{3} \sum_{g_k \in \mathscr{G}} \zeta_{s_u g_k} \cdot (j_i.input + j_i.output)$;
13   Object.setConstraint $(d_{prov} + d_{staging} \leq j_i.ioLimit)$;
    // calculate the availability
14     $t_{exec} \leftarrow \max_{g_k} [\mathscr{R}.\texttt{predict}(j_i, \varepsilon_{g_k} \cdot \zeta_{s_{\{1,2,3\}} g_k})]$;
15     $t_{prov} \leftarrow d_{prov}/bandwidth$;
16     $t_{staging} \leftarrow d_{staging}/bandwidth$;
17   Object.setConstraint $(\frac{t_{exec} + t_{staging}}{t_{exec} + t_{staging} + t_{prov}} \geq \vartheta)$;
18   plan $\leftarrow$ Object.optimize $(t_{exec} + t_{prov} + t_{staging})$;
19   if plan *is null* then
20   repeat j_i;
21   end
22   Submit $(j_i, \mathscr{G}, \text{plan})$;
23   UpdateStates $(\mathscr{G})$;
24 end

Fig. 6.3. Algorithm for searching optimal solutions

6.6.1 Environment Setup

As shown in Fig. 6.4, we adopted three heterogeneous clusters[1] mentioned in the following as target resources. Each cluster is deployed with different grid middleware. The network bandwidth between those clusters is connected by 1 Gbps backbone which is shared by other CERNET research applications nationwide.

---

[1] All implementations for these platforms can be found in different hosting sites. GPE4CGSP, http://grid.hust.edu.cn/; gpe4cgsp/GPE4GTK, http://gpe4gtk.sourceforge.net/; GPE4Unicore, http://www.unicore.eu

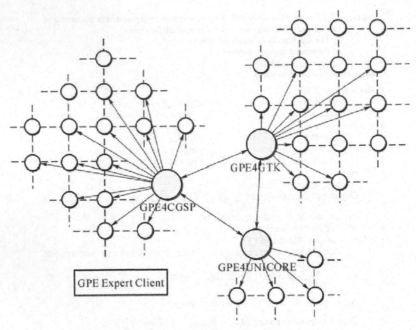

Fig. 6.4.   Experimental environment topology

• *GPE4GTK Cluster*: A cluster of 16 nodes connected by 1 Gbps Ethernet and 10 Gbps Infiniband. Each server in the cluster has a two-way quad Intel Xeon 2.33 GHz processor, 8 GB RAM, 73 GB SAS hard disk. All the servers are equipped with Red Hat Linux Application Server 5 with kernel 2.6.18-8.el5. The Globus Toolkit 4.0.2 is the middleware deployed on the servers.

• *GPE4CGSP Cluster*: A cluster of 16 nodes connected by 1 Gbps Ethernet. Each machine in the cluster has 64 bit four-way 2.0 GHz Xeon processors, 4 GB RAM. All the nodes are equipped with Red Hat Linux with kernel 2.4.20-8. The CGSP v2.0.2 is the default grid middleware for job submission and management.

• *GPE4UNICORE Cluster*: A cluster of 4 servers connected by 1 Gbps Ethernet. Each node has 64 bit quad 2.0 GHz Xeon processors, 4 GB RAM. The operating system deployed on these resources is Red Hat Enterprise Linux Application Server v4 with kernel version 2.6.18. The middleware deployed on the servers is UNICORE 6.0.1.

The JVMs used in the experimental environment are 1.5.0_06-b05 mixed mode (available for X86_32 and X86_64) implemented by SUN for x86 servers. The version of the virtual workspace service is TP1.3. The virtual machine adopted is Xen-3.0.3-9.

These platforms are all encapsulated by Intel's Grid Programming Environment client. Yet the merging work for two releases (i.e., GPE4CGSP and GPE4UNICORE) is not finished. Thus, the initialized parameters were evaluated by the two clients respectively.

6.6.2   Application GridBean

To support the correct execution of the test case, we require the supporting packages, including OpenMPI (version 1.2.5) and image processing toolkits, to be deployed to the target systems. The package size of the virtual machines image and services GAR are 1.1 GB (1.0 GB image file plus 129 MB snapshot file) and 18.0 MB respectively.

The adopted image processing GridBean is developed by the image processing team from ChinaGrid. This GridBean provides more than 20 image rendering algorithms. Domain users can submit the images freely to the grid infrastructure[1]. A suite of test cases is set up to verify our model.

In our experiment, the Gradient and Watershed Segmentation algorithms are adopted to process a remote sensor image. The submitted image can be delivered to 4, 8, 12, 16 nodes for gradient process and 1, 2, 4, 16 nodes for segmentation process respectively. The image size for processing is 21.7 MB. Figs. 6.5(b) to (d) demonstrate the processing procedure and Fig. 6.5(a) is the image processing GridBean.

6.6.3   Abbreviation

The following are the abbreviations that will be used in the rest of the section.
- **DE** denotes the direct execution on specific middleware.
- **VWP** means that the virtual workspace service for provisioning is adopted.
- **DMP** means that dynamical maintenance provisioning is adopted.
- **GTK** is the Globus Toolkit 4.0.2 middleware released by ANL.
- **CGSP** is the ChinaGrid Support Platform 2.0.2 middleware release by ChinaGrid.
- **UNICORE** is the UNICORE 6.0.1 middleware released by UniGrids.

6.6.4   Running Applications Separately on Specific Middleware

At first the benchmark for executing applications on different middleware is evaluated. We ran the two applications on three middlewares from 00:00 to 2:00 am GMT+8 Jan. 18, 2008.

Figs. 6.6 and 6.7 demonstrate the results of the experiment. Figs. 6.6(a) and (c), (b) and (d) denote that when running the image process on two middlewares, CGSP will cost more time but less provisioning time than GTK, respectively.

---

[1] The implementation of Image Processing GridBean can be accessed from http://grid.hust.edu. cn/gpe4cgsp/

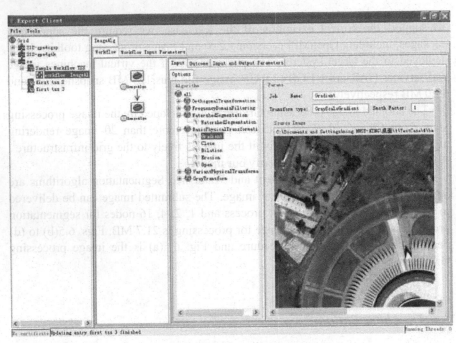

(a) Grid Beans in Expert client

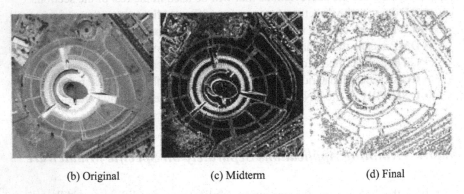

(b) Original   (c) Midterm   (d) Final

Fig. 6.5.   Applications adopted to experiment

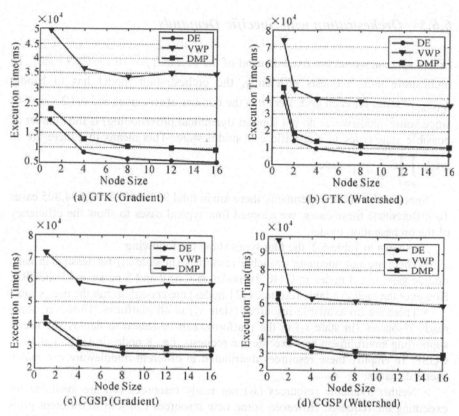

Fig. 6.6. Running the two applications on different platforms with different approaches

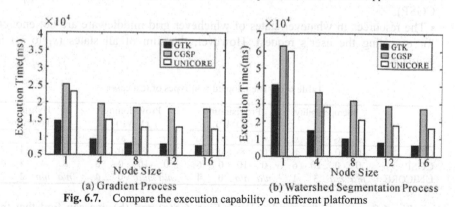

Fig. 6.7. Compare the execution capability on different platforms

Fig. 6.7 presents the execution time on three middlewares as the reference. Obviously, the execution of these systems is different, much due to the different nature and the heterogeneity of physical platforms.

6.6.5 Orchestration with Specific Demands

In this section, we set the fixed demand of the user as $\{ \rho = 16, c = \varnothing, \vartheta = \varnothing \}$. To orchestrate users requests efficiently, the orchestration model has to handle C^n_{m+n-1} states for each grid. Here n is the number of resources and m ($2 \leq m \leq 4$, since some middlewares do not support dynamical provisioning) is the number of possible state types in a specific grid middleware. This means that there are in total $\prod\limits_{g \in G} C^{n_g}_{n_g+m_g-1}$ cases.

Specifically, in our experiment, there are in total $969 \times 969 \times 5 = 4{,}694{,}805$ cases. To differentiate these cases, we adopted four typical cases to·show the efficiency of the orchestration model.

As shown in Table 6.2, the four types show the following:

• There are not adequate available resources (in state s_3) for leasing in each middleware, i.e., 8 nodes in GTK, 10 nodes in CGSP and 3 nodes in UNICORE. However the total available resources (21 nodes) are enough to run the user's job.

• There are no available resources (state s_3) in all platforms. However, some ready resources (in state s_2) in the platforms can be leased to deploy the user's supporting environment and execute the requests, i.e., 8 nodes in GTK and 10 in CGSP. To employ these resources distributed in different middleware can match user's demands.

• Neither available resources (s_3) nor ready resources (s_2) are available for executing the requests. However, some new resources can join in different grids (in state s_1) for computation (i.e., 8 new resources in GTK and 10 new resources in CGSP).

• The resources in whatever states of whichever grid middleware are not enough for executing the user's request. However, the sum of all states (s_1 to s_3) is available.

Table 6.2 The adopted four types of test cases

	Interoperability				Provisioning (DMP)				Provisioning (VWP)				Hybrid orchestration			
	s_1	s_2	s_3	s_4	s_1	s_2	s_3	s_4	s_1	s_2	s_3	s_4	s_1	s_2	s_3	s_4
GTK	0	0	8	8	0	8	0	8	0	8	0	8	4	4	4	4
CGSP	0	0	10	6	0	10	0	6	0	10	0	6	4	4	4	4
UNICORE	n/a	n/a	3	1	n/a	n/a	0	4	n/a	n/a	0	4	n/a	n/a	2	2

Fig. 6.8 presents the results. From Figs. 6.8(a) and (b), we can find that the total execution times of set A to D were longer than the minimal execution on the fast middlewares (GTK). However, the total execution time will not exceed 26,525.04 ms for the gradient process and 27,408.17 ms for the watershed segmentation process. The two durations are near to the slowest execution (26,503.64 ms and 27,373.17 ms respectively). Although the IO costs increase due

to the provisioning (Fig. 6.8(c)), the user's requests and demands are guaranteed. In addition, we can conclude that the adoption of virtual machines provisioning will cost most IOs from Fig. 6.8(c); the interoperation (Set A) costs less IO but needs more time to issue heterogeneous translations.

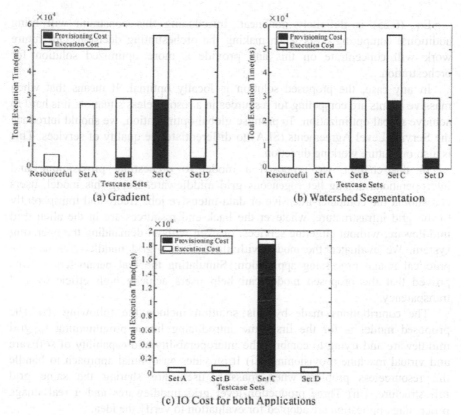

Fig. 6.8. Hybrid orchestration results

6.7 Summary

Although the optimization can help users achieve high efficiency, the user can benefit more if more factors are considered, such as the heterogeneity price. If the adopted resources from the alien grid middleware can provide similar execution attributes, users need not suffer from the *weakest-link effect*. The constraints on heterogeneity can be defined as below.

Constraint 4 (Heterogeneity Price) The heterogeneity is the standard deviation of execution time samples of a job on specific resource $j(r)$. Obviously, the less standard deviation and the shorter execution time is the preference of end users.

$$H = \sqrt{\frac{\sum\limits_{g \in G} \sum\limits_{r \in R(g)} (\overline{t_j^{exec}} - \varepsilon_g \cdot t_{j(r)}^{exec})^2}{\|R\| - 1}} \qquad (6.25)$$

Eq. (6.25) is definitely nonlinear. Introducing this constraint will bring additional computing costs when making the orchestrating decision. Our future work will concentrate on this and provide a more optimized solution for orchestration.

In any case, the proposed solution is locally optimal. It means that when massive clients are competing for resources in a resourceless situation, it is hard to achieve global optimization. To promise global optimization, we should introduce the Service Level Agreements (SLA) to differentiate the quality of services. This is also our future working direction.

In this chapter, we proposed a model to orchestrate provisioning and interoperations among heterogeneous grid middleware. Using this model, users can submit the computer-intensive or data-intensive jobs freely and transparently to the grid infrastructure, whatever the back end resources are in the alien grid middleware, without targeting services, or even without demanding the operating system. We evaluated the model with three known grid middlewares using a practical image processing application. Simulating the real parameters, results proved that the proposed model can help users achieve high efficiency and transparency.

The contributions made by this solution include the following: (i) The proposed model is for the first time introducing linear programming to grid middleware and trying to combine the interoperability and capability of software and virtual machine provisioning. (ii) It provides an optimal approach to handle the resourceless problem when massive users are sharing the same grid infrastructure. (iii) Three production-level grid middlewares and a real image processing application are adopted for evaluation to verify the idea.

References

Davidovi' T, Liberti L, Maculan N, Mladenovi' N (2007) Towards the optimal solution of the multiprocessor scheduling problem with communication delays. In: 3rd Multidisciplinary Int. Conf. on Scheduling: Theory and Application. Paris, France, pp. 128-135.

Drozdowski M (1996) Scheduling multiprocessor tasks—an overview. European Journal of Operational Research, 94: 215-230.

Erwin DW (2002) Unicore—a grid computing environment. Concurrency and Computation-Practice & Experience, 14(13-15): 1395-1410.

Foster I (2006) Globus toolkit version 4: Software for service-oriented systems.

Journal of Computer Science and Technology, 21(4): 513-520.

Gentzsch W (2001) Sun grid engine: Towards creating a compute power grid. First IEEE/ACM International Symposium on Cluster Computing and the Grid, 2001, pp. 35-36.

Gong Y, Dong F, Li W, Xu Z (2003) Vega infrastructure for resource discovery in grids. J Comput Sci Technol, 18(4): 413-422.

Sun H, Liu W, Wo T, Hu C (2006) Crown node server: An enhanced grid service container based on gt4 wsrf core. In: 5th International Conference on Grid and Cooperative Computing Workshops, 2006. IEEE Computer Society, Changsha, China, pp. 510-517.

Jin H (2004) Chinagrid: Making grid computing a reality. In: Chen Z, Chen H, Miao Q, Fu Y, Fox E, Lim E (eds.) Digital Libraries: International Collaboration and Cross-Fertilization. Springer, Singapore, pp. 13-24.

Jin H, Qi L, Wu S, Luo Y, Dai J (2007) Dependency-aware maintenance for dynamic grid services. In: Li J, Zhang X (eds.) The 39th International Conference on Parallel Processing, 2007. IEEE Computer Society, Xi'an, China, pp. 64-71.

Keahey K, Foster I, Freeman T, Zhang XH, Galron D (2005) Virtual workspaces in the grid. Euro-Par 2005 Parallel Processing. 3648: 421-431.

Maculan N, Ribeiro CC, Porto S, de Souza CC (1999) A new formulation for scheduling unrelated processors under precedence constraints. RAIRO Operations Research, 33: 87-90.

Munro C, Koblitz B, Santos N, Khan A (2006) Measurement of the lcg2 and glite file catalogue's performance. IEEE Transactions on Nuclear Science, 53(4): 2228-2232.

Open Grid Forum (2005) Gin interoperation now project. URL https://forge.gridforum.org/projects/gin.

Qi L, Jin H, Foster I, Gawor J (2007) Hand: Highly available dynamic deployment infrastructure for globus toolkit 4. In: Vecchia GD, di Serafino D, Marra I, Perla F (eds.) 15th Euromicro International Conference on Parallel, Distributed and Network-Based Processing (PDP 2007). IEEE Computer Society, Naples, Italy, pp. 155-162.

Ratering R, Lukichev A, Riedel M, Mallmann D, Vanni A, Cacciari C, Lanzarini S, Benedyczak K, Borcz M, Kluszcynski R, Bala P, Ohme G (2006) Gridbeans: Support e-Science and grid applications. In: 2nd IEEE International Conference on e-Science and Grid Computing, 2006. e-Science'06, IEEE Computer Society, Amsterdam, The Netherlands, pp. 45-45.

Smith M, Friese T, Freisleben B (2004) Towards a service-oriented ad hoc grid. In: 3rd International Workshop on Parallel and Distributed Computing, 2004. 3rd International Symposium on/Algorithms, Models and Tools for Parallel Computing on Heterogeneous Networks, 2004. IEEE Computer Society, Cork, Ireland, pp. 201-208.

Snelling D, Berghe Svd, Laszewski Gv, Wieder P, Breuer D, MacLaren J, Nicole D, Hoppe H (2002) A UNICORE gloubs interoperability layer. Computing and Informatics, 21: 399-411.

Weissman JB, Kim S, England D (2005) A framework for dynamic service adaptation in the grid: Next generation software program progress report. In: 19th IEEE International Parallel and Distributed Processing Symposium, 2005. IEEE Computer Society, Denver, CA, USA, p. 5.

Wu Y, Wu S, Yu H, Hu C (2005) Cgsp: An extensible and reconfigurable grid framework. In: Yang LT (ed.) The 6th International Workshop on Advanced Parallel Processing Technologies. Springer, Hong Kong, China, pp. 292-300.

Implementation of Dynamic Provisioning with Community Services

Abstract: In the earlier chapters we explored the provisioning technology in terms of infrastructure, architecture, model and strategies. Combined with these features, we implemented the Guardian system to help the administrators, developers and end users to provision applications on ChinaGrid. After exploring the implementation details and actual workflow, readers can understand more about the service-oriented provisioning system. Furthermore, we will introduce practical applications that apply provisioning technologies to improve the efficiency and availability. These applications have been deployed on ChinaGrid.

7.1 Introduction

According to the discussion in earlier chapters, we can conclude that the features of provisioning for service-oriented applications are as follows.

• *Simple Installation of Packages*: Similar to the traditional installing packages (e.g. tar balls-.tar.gz, Microsoft installer-.msi, RPM package manager-.rpm and so forth), the installation of Web services is normally to copy service packages (e.g. Web archives-.war, grid archives-.gar and enterprize archives-.ear) to the service containers. The services package consists of Web Service Deployment Descriptor (WSDD), Web Service Description Languages (WSDL) and their binary implementations. Normally the size of services packages is far less than that of traditional installing packages.

• *Uniform Hosting Environment*: Unlike the traditional binary program, the service-oriented applications are running in a service engine (e.g. Axis 1.4 (2006), Axis 2 (2008) and XFire (Codehaus, 2008)) within a container (e.g. Globus Toolkit 4) (Foster, 2006), Tomcat (Apache Tomcat, 2007) and jBoss (Reverbel *et al.*, 2004)) that supports the same open standard instead of running directly in the operating system. Developers and end users can develop and use Web services under a common specifications framework. Thus the Web services can easily shield the heterogeneity of resources.

• *Highly Integrating Capability*: Different from the traditional communication approaches between processes (e.g. pipe line, network socket and so forth), the Web services communicate with each other by using Simple Object Access Protocol (SOAP). Associating with Universal Description, Discovery and Integration (UDDI), Web services are born of coupling and composing components.

Combined with the concentrations of the provisioning system, we can conclude that the design goals include the following items:

• *Role-Oriented Maintenance*: From the lifecycle of Web services, ChinaGrid has three classes of role: services developers, system administrators and domain experts. As a service-oriented maintenance system, Guardian was designed to accommodate all types. Differentiating the user interface for the three types of users allows us to improve both security and convenience. Service developers use Guardian to deploy the under development services modules for testing and evaluation purposes. Thus the services deployed by developers should have constrained accessibility and could be automatically torn down by the maintenance system when they have arrived. On the other hand, Guardian should provide convenience for domain experts to customize the accessibility of SOA infrastructure, the lifecycle of services components and scalability of containers on demand. Finally, system administrators need to access all the information and privileges of all the maintenance procedures and logs. Moreover, the system administrator should be able to understand the more detailed deployment attributes.

• *Transparency in Heterogeneity and Dependencies*: One problem with a service-oriented distributed system such as a grid is the daily growth in users, services and resources. The complicated relationship among these entities and the heterogeneous nature of resources bring challenges for system maintenance. With Guardian, we wanted to make executing a maintenance as easy as possible so that developers, end users and administrators alike can finish maintenance quickly through the administration console. Our interfaces are designed to be intuitive so that they can be used without having to waste time understanding the dependencies among resources and the characteristics of heterogeneous resources.

• *Tolerance of Transient Failures*: Since the runtime of highly distributed systems is rather unpredictable, many transient failures bring risks to the maintenance system. For example, networking latency or maintaining targets being temporarily offline will delay or even cause global maintenance to fail eventually. It is necessary that the maintenance system should have the capability to tolerate transient failures and correctly continue with paused maintenances when targets are available again. In addition, Guardian should also process the inconsistencies (e.g. missed patches for critical services, invalid maintaining status, and so forth) even when the maintaining targets have suffered a relatively long break.

• *High Availability for Multi-VO Applications*: Guardian's main goal is to provide a maintenance for flexible and highly available serving of multi-VO applications. With the increase in VO users and VO applications, the availability of a global infrastructure should be guaranteed when massive users frequently activate or shut down their own application services. This motivation requires Guardian to detect the runtime status of the shared infrastructure, report this to the maintenance system and correctly execute the maintenances as fast as possible according to the status of the maintaining target.

7.2 Implementation of Essential Components

A complete Guardian system consists of five main components as follows:
- A repository that stores Web service packages and associated metadata;
- A set of client tools that are used in each Guardian administration console to manage SOA infrastructure by interacting either directly with the Guardian provisioning service or through the maintenance worker when it is available. In addition, inside the administration console, the tag management tool that allows multiple users to identify their resources with tags according to the requirements of deployed applications;
- A front end provisioning service named as virtual maintainer that is responsible for decoupling the end users' maintenances into atomic or smaller ones, optimizing the maintenances and storing the atomic maintenances in a global maintenance stack;
- A set of maintenance workers that executes the maintenances stored in the global tasks separately for each resource synchronously or asynchronously;
- And a set of probes are implemented as AXIS handler deployed on each end resource. These probes are in charge of recording the runtime invocation dependencies and interacting with maintenance workers upon the runtime status to decide when to activate related maintenances.

7.2.1 Service Repository

The service repository's main task is to serve service package files much like a normal Web server. However, the service repository is optimized to efficiently serve packages from, and provide packages to, the client. Firstly, it introduces an efficient role-oriented secure policy to guarantee the safety of uploaded packages. Secondly, Guardian service repository can choose the traditional FTP server and HTTP server, ChinaGrid Support Platform's virtual space services (Wu *et al.*, 2007) and GridFTP (Allcock *et al.*, 2005) server as the repository server according to the different requirements. After adopting a suitable approach, the service repository makes service packages available via different efficient transfer mechanisms such as HTTP. Finally, the service repository analyzes the uploaded dependent library (i.e., Jar files) and WSDD, parses out the dependent services classes and registers them in services' metadata.

• *Role-Oriented Security*: The Grid Security Infrastructure (GSI) (Welch, 2004) authentication and authorization are used to ensure that only authorized users can invoke the uploading operations. Each user should use his private key signing packages and transfer them to the service repository. According to the user roles, the certifications are also classified in three types: the developer certificates are authorized in a limited period for uploading and deploying privileges; the domain experts are similar to developers but their proxies could be renewed on demand for accessing privilege (using **grid-proxy-init** in simple CA toolkits of the Globus toolkit); the system administrator's certificates are valid all the time. However, execution of critical operations (such as deletion of service packages) needs double confirmation.

• *Redundant Transferring Mechanism*: According to the criteria in Chapter 2, the Guardian service repository guarantees enough redundant approaches for accessing stored service packages. Currently it supports HTTP (http://) and FTP (ftp://) protocols, GridFTP (gsiftp://) protocol, CGSP's file transferring protocol (vs://) and the DIME attachment in SOAP message. Domain experts or developers can specify demanded transfer protocols by invoking **guardian-reposit-upload** inside their own program and **download** function inside **DeployService** that is normally deployed with Guardian probes in the physical resources. Naturally, support of GridFTP and CGSP virtual space services require running GridFTP daemon **globus-gridftp-server** and **gridftp_update_start** to provide storage services respectively.

• *Registry of Services' Metadata*: For convenience in recording the related classes and dynamic dependencies, service repository will parse the WSDD and Jar files inside Grid Archive (GAR) or Web Archive (WAR). It retrieves the service name, service class name and associated classes list. Furthermore, it records them into a hash map. The information can help the dependency probes analyze invocation dependencies.

7.2.2   Administration Console Client

As shown in Fig. 7.1, the administration console client allows Guardian users to manage their services on rented containers without the need to contact them directly. The administration console clients typically run on the user's desktop machine. They are used to manually upload and register service packages to the service repository (Fig. 7.1(a)), deliver the maintenance tasks to the virtual maintainer by dragging and dropping icons and monitor the state of each maintenance (Fig. 7.1(b)) and runtime dependencies among services on different containers (Fig. 7.1(c)). Naturally, users can pause, resume or even cancel the scheduled atomic maintenances on each container. Once users or administrators submit the service packages to the Guardian system, the dependency parser will parse all of the related classes from the library file and WSDD. In addition, all the submitted maintenance tasks for the SOA infrastructure will be scheduled and executed adaptively according to different states of the target container. During the runtime, all of the invocation dependencies among the services will be recorded automatically by Guardian probes. By recording those dependencies, Guardian workers finish the maintenances more safely and accurately.

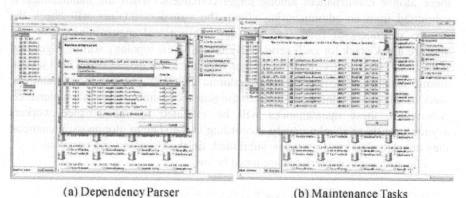

(a) Dependency Parser   (b) Maintenance Tasks

(c) Dependency Detection

Fig. 7.1.   Guardian administration console

7.2.3 *Virtual Maintainer*

The virtual maintainer discussed in Chapter 5 is the facade of the Guardian system. It is in charge of analyzing the maintenances from users, atomizing the maintenances into a unique sequence for each target container and orchestrating these atomic maintenances among target containers. When the maintenance is submitted from an administrating client, the virtual maintainer will check the service dependencies first, find out the implicational maintaining tasks and allocate a task stack for each service. By invoking the topology sorting algorithm (Qi *et al.*, 2007), the virtual maintainer decouples the maintenance into several atomic maintenances. It pushes these atomic maintenances into the maintaining stack of related containers and updates the sequence number of each maintenance. Afterwards, these maintenances will be executed by maintenance workers asynchronously or synchronously. According to the state of atomic maintenances, they are classified into four types: submitted, finished, running and canceled.

The main service interfaces are listed below.

```
public interface ivirtualMaintainer {
    public int vdeploy (VdeployRequest request);
    public int deleteOperation
            (DeleteOperationRequest delRequest);
    public CheckOperationResponse checkOperations
            (CheckOperationRequest request);
}
```

The **vdeploy** function is for submitting maintenance tasks. It will return **0** if the submitted maintenance task is successfully decoupled; the **deleteOperation** is for canceling scheduled atomic maintenances; **checkOperations** is to get the state of scheduled atomic maintenances.

7.2.4 *Maintenance Workers*

Maintenance workers are actual executors to run atomic maintenances stored in the maintenance stack. The main responsibility of these workers includes (i) responding to the μ-query requests from the end dependency probes (see Section 5.2), (ii) activating the service repository to transfer the related services packages to target containers and (iii) invoking the DeployService synchronously or asynchronously to finish atomic maintenances on a remote container.

• *μ-Query Service*: This service is working in asynchronous mode (see Chapter 5). Once a normal request arrives at the end container, the deployed Guardian probes (implemented as an AXIS handler) will query **versionUpgrade** interface with the local maintenance ID (*localId*) to confirm whether the requested services on that container need maintenance. The Guardian worker checks the latest maintenance sequence number (*globalId*) in the maintenance stack for the related services on the container. The *globalId* will return to Guardian probes. In addition, if *globalId* > *localId*, Guardian worker will sequentially activate the maintenances on that container till the containers' *localId* is equal to *globalId*.

    • *Activating Repository Transfer and Remote Maintenance*: In asynchronous mode, once μ-query service has made the maintaining decisions, Guardian worker will communicate with the service repository and start transferring packages to the target containers. Maintenance workers will wait till all the necessary packages are transferred completely. Sequentially, it delivers a message to the remote containers' **DeployService** and begins to start the maintenances one by one till the *localId* stored in the remote container matches the latest sequence stored in the virtual maintainer. On the other hand, in synchronous mode, maintenance workers directly contact the service repository and the remote containers to start the maintenance in the meantime.

    When the managed resources and users are on an unpredictable scale, the maintenance workers in the asynchronous mode will create a bottleneck in the Guardian system, since the frequent μ requests from all the probes will eventually crash the whole maintenance system. We take two precautions to lower the negative effects of this problem:

    • *Building a Worker Pool*: When the throughput of μ-requests is on a lower level, the number of maintenance workers will be constrained. With the request throughput increasing, the maintenance worker pool will automatically initiate more workers to handle it. Once a worker finishes the assigned tasks, it will return to the pool and wait for a new assignment.

    • *Designing a Postponing Mechanism in Guardian Probes*: This approach tries to reduce the access rate of μ-requests. Setting a cache counter in the dependency probes, only if the value of the counter achieves a threshols, the probe will deliver a request to the μ-service in a maintenance worker. Naturally, this approach needs cooperation with the synchronous mode, because the missed μ-requests could disturb the upper business logic if the maintenances are submitted between the countering gaps.

7.2.5 Dependency Probes

The Guardian probes process delivers μ-requests to maintenance workers, records the invocation dependencies and responds to the maintenance workers' maintenances.

    The probe functionality is implemented by three AXIS handlers (as shown in Fig. 7.2). The **GuardianHandler** in the response flow (defined in **server-config.wsdd**) of AXIS is in charge of delivering the μ-requests to the maintenance workers once the normal requests arrive.

```
client-config.wsdd Request flow:
    <handler
        type="java:cn.edu.chinagrid.wsrf.handlers.ClientDependencyHandler"/>

server-config.wsdd Response flow:
    <handler
        type="java:cn.edu.chinagrid.wsrf.handlers.ServerDependencyHandler"/>
Request flow:
    <handler
        type="java:cn.edu.chinagrid.wsrf.handlers.GuardianHandler"/>
```

Fig. 7.2. AXIS handlers for invocation dependency detection

Since the probes are dependent on μ-query services deployed on the maintenance workers, the maintenance workers will, in addition, invoke the **DeployService** on the destination container. Therefore, the probes are designed to ignore these invocation messages (i.e., messages to DeployService and μ-query service). This approach can avoid deadlocks due to possible circular invocations.

On the other hand, the **ClientDependencyHandler** and **ServiceDependencyHandler** are a pair deployed in the request flow of **client-conFig. wsdd** and the response flow of **server-conFig. wsdd** inside the HAND infrastructure (see Chapter 2) respectively. First, the former handler invokes the **Thread.getStackTrace()** operation when the source service instance is invoking another service. Furthermore, client handler retrieves a possible service class from the current calling stack in JVM and records the necessary information (e.g. the source IP address, serving port and issued service class name, as shown in Fig. 7.3) in the SOAP header. Sequentially, when the delivered message arrives at the target container, the latter handler can detect invocation dependencies upon the marked metadata. In this way, the Guardian system can dynamically detect the runtime invocation dependency. Thus the maintenance workers can hold onto the depending invocations temporally. Accordingly, Guardian improved the global availability and guaranteed the accuracy of maintenances.

Typically, the probe runs on each container that is managed by the Guardian system; however, there may be some cases where the probes are not deployed on the container, such as in a newly joined plain AXIS container. In the case where no probe is running or the probe process fails, the maintenance workers communicate directly with the **DeployService** that is the default system service of a CGSP container. Nevertheless, the invocation dependencies will be ignored.

7.2.6 *Working Flow*

This section illustrates how the Guardian components work together to manage the packages used by the earlier example in which an administrator installs an updated version of the execution service package on an SOA infrastructure for the image virtual organization (Image-VO) which demands this upgrade on several containers.

```
<?xml version="1.0" encoding="UTF-8" ?>
<soapenv:Envelope
  xmlns:soapenv="http://schemas.xmlsoap.org/soap/envelope/"
  xmlns:xsd="http://www.w3.org/2001/XMLSchema"
  xmlns:xsi="http://www.w3.org/2001/XMLSchema-instance"
  xmlns:wsa="http://schemas.xmlsoap.org/ws/2004/03/addressing">
<soapenv:Header>
<wsa:MessageID>uuid:174b4570-7b3e-11dc-9118-fee1ae4401b2</wsa:MessageID>
<wsa:To>
  http://211.69.198.250:8080/wsrf/services/guardian/invocation
</wsa:To>
<wsa:Action>
  http://chinagrid.hust.edu.cn/namespaces/guardian/invocation\\
                          /invocationPortType/invokeRequest
</wsa:Action>
<wsa:From>
  <wsa:Address>
    http://schemas.xmlsoap.org/ws/2004/03/addressing/role/anonymous
  </wsa:Address>
</wsa:From>
 <dependencyService
className="cn.edu.chinagrid.guardian.invocation.Invocation"
ipAddress="211.69.198.121" port="8080" xmlns="" >
</soapenv:Header>
<soapenv:Body>
  <InvocationRequest
    xmlns="http://chinagrid.hust.edu.cn/namespaces/guardian/invocation">
    <msg>pingValidity</msg>
  </InvocationRequest>
</soapenv:Body>
</soapenv:Envelope>
```

Fig. 7.3. The SOAP message processed by Guardian probes

(i) The administrator logs into the administration console by using his private key. The administration console lists all available containers and service packages.

(ii) He drags the new version of the execution service package from a local folder to a services package view of the administration console. Afterwards, the administration console requests a remote service repository for authentication.

(iii) After authentication, the package of local services is transferred to the service repository by invoking **guardian-reposit-upload** function. The transferring protocol is configured in **gui.conFig.xml** and FTP is the default. Before transferring, the repository checks the package file to see whether it exists in the administrator's directory according to its MD5 code. If it does, an error message will be generated to alert the user.

(iv) After transferring the service packages, the repository's registry module begins to untar service packages, retrieves WSDD and related library (i.e., Jar files). Then, all of the metadata about the uploaded services (including service name, service class name, owner and depended classes stack) are stored in the registry center. After registering and validating the metadata, the repository makes the uploaded package available for downloading. Furthermore, the confirmed information is returned to the administration console (Fig. 7.1(a)).

(v) Sequentially, the administrator selects all of the containers according to their tags attribute (i.e., tagged as Image-VO) and drags the execution service package icon from service package view to the container view. The administration console packs the related service packages and containers as a maintenance task request and delivers it to the virtual maintainer's EPR and invokes **vdeploy** function.

(vi) The virtual maintainer executes a topology sorting algorithm upon the delivered maintenances, mines the dependency map and finds out implicational maintenance from the information services and data center service. Furthermore, it feeds back the complete atomic maintenances list to the administration console (Fig. 7.1(b)) for confirmation.

(vii) According to the fed information, the administrator adjusts related atomic maintenances and decides to execute the maintenances in asynchronous mode or synchronous mode.

(viii) In the synchronous mode, the console delivers an activating instruction directly to the maintenance workers. The maintenance worker pool will assign the maintenance to an available worker. The worker verifies the administrator's credential and confirms if the administrator has the privilege to execute the maintenances.

(ix) The maintenance worker invokes **checkOperations** function provided by the virtual maintainer to pop out a submitted maintenance task from the maintenance stack. Sequentially, it informs the service repository to transfer required services packages to target containers. Furthermore, it invokes the **deploy** function of **DeployService** in remote containers. The communication between the maintenance workers, repository and destination containers uses a uniform system authentication.

(x) The maintenance worker repeats step 9 until it finishes all of the atomic maintenances. The synchronous maintenance ends.

(xi) In the asynchronous mode, the administration console advises that the maintenances have been scheduled. Meanwhile, the domain users can begin to use the prepared containers.

(xii) The VO application delivers normal requests to the ready containers that had deployed the execution services. When the normal requests arrive, the dependency probe (**GuardianHandler**) intercepts and captures the request information and adjudges whether the cache counter has arrived at the threshold. If it is lower than the threshold, the requests will be passed into the AXIS engine. Otherwise, it sends a μ-request to the maintenance worker with *localId*.

(xiii) The maintenance worker checks the latest maintenance ID (*globalId*) for the execution service for the target container and compares it with *localId* in μ-requests. If *globalId* = *localId*, the maintenance worker returns guardian-maintenance-none to the dependency probe and lets it continue processing original requests. However, if *globalId* > *localId*, and invocation dependencies are ready for further operations, the maintenance worker returns guardian-maintenance-required back to dependency probe, lets it stop processing normal requests temporally, pops up maintenances from *localId* and executes a similar operation to step 9.

(xiv) The maintenance worker repeats the execution of step 13 until the target containers' *localId* is equal to requested services' *globalId*. Sequentially, the dependency probe passes the requested message to AXIS engine and continues the upper business logic. The asynchronous maintenance ends. Furthermore, the maintenance worker will be queued back into the worker pool.

(xv) The **ServiceDependencyHandler** and **ClientDependencyHandler** in the Guardian probe record the invocation dependencies in runtime for reference of future maintenances (Fig. 7.1(c)).

(xvi) If the assigned lifecycle duly arrives and the user does not renew the services, the virtual maintainer will construct an undeployment and a destroy maintenance for the deployed execution service, information service and transferring service. Afterwards, a maintenance worker will be activated to execute the destruction maintenances in synchronous mode.

7.2.7 Lessons

In asynchronous mode, the Guardian system can't promise that each maintenance for heterogeneous resources is finished in a predictable time because the virtual maintainer and Guardian workers are working asynchronously. Hence, if an application demands that the maintenances should finish completely on all related resources before the later tasks, it will benefit little from the asynchronous mode. In addition, the application clients may wait for a long time if they request a new service on resources which accumulated a list of maintenances. In this case, the client-tier may need a fault tolerant mechanism to avoid possible losses from the first access. The feedback mechanism provided by Guardian (see Section 4.5) can help the client application achieve the maintenance states at runtime.

Otherwise, compared with the traditional distributed provisioning system, Guardian is not appropriate for maintenance on the hardware or operating system. Because these fundamental upgrades need rebooting the system, the probes in the target resources are forbidden to obtain super privileges. In addition, there is no promise that the system can correctly come back online after these operations.

Finally, the memory used by the Guardian workers implementation grows linearly with the number of maintaining requests. To address this, an archive mechanism is proposed to place the pending tasks in a database system or a dumping file. If some planned maintenances are not requested for a fixed period, these tasks will be dumped from the Guardian workers's memory into a local file or a database record. The specific period is configured by users from the administration console. If some new requests arrive in the end resources that are for the archived maintenance, the responding Guardian worker will load them from archived media and deliver related atomic maintenance to the target platform. In this way, for the Guardian system to run out of memory can be avoided over a long period.

7.3 Community Services that Apply the Dynamic Provisioning System

In this section, we will introduce the community services that apply the dynamic provisioning system in the ChinaGrid project.

7.3.1 Bioinformatic Services

Bioinformatics (He *et al.*, 2004) is an emerging field that contains biological information acquisition, processing, storage, distribution, analysis and explanations of all aspects, including its comprehensive use of mathematics, computer science and biology tools to clarify and understand large amounts of data containing biological significance. Traditionally, bioinformatics research and the support of the infrastructure are geographically distributed. In addition, research institutes built their own research platform, including computing, software, storage and instrument resources. Sequentially, the use of these resources is relatively low. Moreover, there are many bioinformatics researchers who eagerly pursue those resources to support their research work.

To resolve this problem, the ChinaGrid team built the Bioinformatics Grid to efficiently organize and share the biologically related resources distributed in the universities. It has integrated 16 major computing clusters distributed in 6 top universities in China. By efficiently providing more than 120 bioinformatic services (as shown in Table 7.1), scientists can easily deploy their interested application and collect the simulation data from the shared public resources. Today there are more than 50,000 researchers who fetch their research results from the bioinformatic grid.

7.3.2 Image Processing Services

There are three typical applications in the ChinaGrid project to hire an image processing grid to complete their complicated tasks. These applications are the visual human project, remote sensing and medical image analysis (Zheng *et al.*, 2004).

• *Visual Human Project* (VHP), an outgrowth of the NLM's 1986 Long-Range Plan, concentrates on producing a system of knowledge structures that will transparently link visual knowledge forms to symbolic knowledge formats, such as the names of body parts. To perform registration, segmentation and 3D rendering on the client side in an open service perspective, the VHP in ChinaGrid demands much computation and storage resources in a dynamical approach. The major services deployed by VHP include (i) high profile body data acquisition, (ii) runtime computations for body image rotation, cutting, zooming and hiding, and (iii) a design model of human body organs.

Table 7.1   Shared bioinformatic services

Services category	Software packages
SARS related software	PCR
	PClustal W
	Clustal W
	Protein docking (Gramm)
	Protein structural analysis(Interproscan, cog, pdb)
Dna sequence assembly services	Euler
	Phrap
	Phred
	Cross_match
	Cap3
	Tigr
Dna sequence alignment services	ATGC
	PClustal W
	Blast
	Fasta
	Clustal W
	Mumer
	mpiBlast
Sequence analysis services	Genscan
	Glimmer
	Glimmer M
	TransTerm
	RepeatMasker
	RepeatFinder
	Cpgplot
	StackPack
	sirnaPro
	EMBOSS package
	BLAST
	ClustalW
	MyBlast
Protein analysis service	Interproscan
Molecular dynamics	SAM/HMMer
	Modeller/Prospect
	AMBER/GROMACS
	Procheck
	CE/CE-MC
Gene analysis services	GeneKey
	EDSAc
Other services	Phlip
	Paml
	DCGene

• *Remote Sensing Technologies* have been widely applied in earth observation, natural resource management and weather prediction. Normally, the remote sensing applications collect the data from various devices (e.g. aircraft, satellites or ships), process the original data and present the data in a friendly way to users. In order to create sensor-based maps, most remote sensing systems need to extrapolate sensor data in relation to a reference point including distances between known points on the ground. Several fundamental image processing services are necessary for remote sensing.

• *Medical Image Analysis* has more complicated requirements of the computation infrastructure. By using the image processing grid, medical image analyzing applications can quickly compare the patient's medical images by type-B ultrasonic and X-ray check against specific diseases, to help doctors make decisions.

Until now, there are in total 14 classes, 35 services available for domain experts to deploy for different usage. By accessing these services, the three hospitals affiliated to Sun Yat-Sen University have processed at least 100,000 medical images and generated 10,000 medical reports for the patients.

7.3.3   Massive Data Processing Services

The goal of a massive information processing grid is to provide access for a particular application of a consistent interface to create efficient mass data sharing and a collaboration environment in a distributed heterogeneous grid environment with massive data resources including storage and data. In ChinaGrid, three applications are deployed on massive data processing services.

• *University Digital Museum Grid* (UDMGrid) (Chen *et al.*, 2007; 2006; 2008): Since the multi-disciplinary resources at digital museums in China are isolated and dispersed without sufficient interconnection, UDMGrid integrates the enormous dispersed resources of various digital museums, to share the resources effectively and eliminate the information island, to filter and classify the collection information and to provide an appropriate information service to users according to their knowledge levels and motivation, through a unified grid portal.

• *High Energy Physics Computing Grid* (HEPGrid): The focus of HEPGrid is to help Chinese physicists process the data from the Cosmic Ray ASy experiment in Tibet, ARGO experiment, Alpha Magnetic Spectrometer and Beijing Spectrometer Collaboration.

• *Access Grid for ChinaGrid* (AG4ChinaGrid): AG4ChinaGrid is a collaboration platform to coordinate the human resources and computation resources distributed geographically.

Currently, the massive data processing grid connects 18 digital museums in 10 cities and integrates at least 100,000 digital samples.

7.3.4   CFD Grid

The Computational Fluid Dynamics Grid provides a grid environment for different

CFD applications which need high performance computing (Lin *et al.*, 2004).

• *The Optimal Design Of Aircraft Systems*: By applying a Fuzzy Genetic Algorithm, the optimal design aircraft systems requests a collection of mathematics services to complete complex iterative calculations.

• *Powder Compaction and Flowing Process*: Powder metallurgy is an advanced materials technology that has been widely applied in the volume production of mechanical parts with high performance and precision. As one of the main procedures in the process, the compaction procedure is in charge of forming the shape of the products. To optimize this procedure, many complicated nonlinear factors are used. CFD Grid provides parallel computation and storage resources to complete the nonlinear analysis.

• *Parallel Molecular Dynamics*: This is also an example of typical optimization applications that hire grid and distributed resources to achieve a better molecular dynamics parallel algorithm.

7.4 Summary

After introducing the infrastructure, architecture, asynchronous models and scheduling strategies, we demonstrate the engineering implementation and practical applications in this chapter. By using state of the art Web service middleware and friendly user interfaces, our Guardian system can dynamically provision applications to ChinaGrid according to user's, administrator's or developer's demands. It can detect the dependencies during the runtime. Furthermore, both synchronous and asynchronous provisioning models are embedded in the Guardian provisioning system. Different users can freely deploy, undeploy and reconfigure their domain applications on demand to the ChinaGrid infrastructure. As a fundamental function of CGSP middleware, the dynamical provisioning function has been widely applied in the bioinformatic grid, image processing grid, massive data processing grid and the CFD Grid within the ChinaGrid.

References

Allcock W, Bresnahan J, Kettimuthu R, Link M, Dumitrescu C, Raicu I, Foster I (2005) The globus striped gridftp framework and server. In: IEEE/ACM International Conference on Super Computing 2005. IEEE Computer Society, Cambridge, Massachusetts, USA, pp. 54-62.

Apache Tomcat (2007) Tomcat frequently asked questions documentation. Http://tomcat.apache.org/faq/deployment.html.

Axis 1.4 (2006) Apache axis 1.4. http://ws.apache.org/axis/.

Axis 2 (2008) Apache axis 2. URL http://ws.apache.org/axis2/.

Chen X, Ou H, Luo X, Chen M, Zhang Y, Hao K, Mi S (2006) The progress of university digital museum grid. In: GCCW '06: Proceedings of the 5th International Conference on Grid and Cooperative Computing Workshops. IEEE Computer Society, Washington, DC, USA, pp. 78-85.

Chen M, Chen X, Luo X (2007) Brief account of multilayer portal model for information grid. In: InfoScale '07: Proceedings of the 2nd International Conference on Scalable Information Systems. ICST (Institute for Computer Sciences, Social-Informatics and Telecommunications Engineering), Brussels, Belgium, pp. 1-2.

Chen X, Chen M, Luo X (2008) A multilayer portal model for information grid. In: CHINAGRID '08: Proceedings of the 3rd ChinaGrid Annual Conference (ChinaGrid 2008). IEEE Computer Society, Washington, DC, USA, pp. 78-85.

Codehaus (2008) Xfire project(aka. cxf). http://xfire.codehaus.org.

Foster I (2006) Globus toolkit version 4: Software for service-oriented systems. Journal of Computer Science and Technology, 21(4): 513-520.

He K, Dong S, Du Z, Cao Y, Zhang L (2004) A grid-enabled pipeline for sirna design. In: The 2004 International Conference on Parallel and Distributed Processing Techniques and Applications. Las Vegas, USA.

Lin X, Sun X, Lu X, Deng Q, Li M, Liu H, Qi Y, Chen L (2004) Recent advances in cfd grid application platform. In: SCC '04: Proceedings of the 2004 IEEE International Conference on Services Computing. IEEE Computer Society, Washington, DC, USA, pp. 588-591.

Qi L, Jin H, Luo Y, Shi X, Wang C (2007) Service dependency model for dynamic and stateful grid services. In: Jin H (ed.) The 7th International Conference on Algorithms and Architectures for Parallel Processing. Springer Verlag, Hangzhou, China, pp. 278-289.

Reverbel F, Burke B, Fleury M (2004) Dynamic deployment of iiop-enabled components in the jboss server. In: Emmerich W, Wolf AL (eds.) 2nd International Working Conference on Component Deployment. Springer, Edinburgh, UK, pp. 65-80.

Welch V (2004) Globus toolkit version 4 grid security infrastructure: A standards perspective. URL http://www-unix.globus.org/toolkit/docs/development/4.0-drafts/security/GT4-GSI-Overview.pdf.

Wu S, Jin H, Xiong M, Wang W (2007) Data management services and transfer scheme in Chinagrid. Int J Web Grid Serv, 3(4): 447-461.

Zheng R, Jin H, Zhang Q, Li Y, Chen J (2004) Ipge: Image processing grid environment using components and workflow techniques. In: Jin H, Pan Y, Xiao N, Sun J (eds.) Grid and Cooperative Computing 2004. Lecture Notes in Computer Science, Vol. 3251, Springer Berlin, Heidelberg, pp. 671-678.

8

Conclusions and Future Challenges

Abstract: With the rapid development of a distributed computing system, an efficient and effective provisioning system is necessary to help different users easily access unlimited computing or storage power. This chapter reviews the whole book and concludes the contribution of our studies.

8.1   Conclusions

After years of research and development, grid computing has become a mature and widely applied technology. Currently, a large number of grid nodes have been deployed to serve scientific applications such as bioinformatics, image processing and massive data processing. Obviously, the grid has made important contributions to these fields. However, with continuous growth in the grid scale, efficient and effective approaches to maintaining the grid infrastructure are more and more important and popular. In particular, how does the grid infrastructure handle the conflicts between the demands of high availability from end users and efficient maintenance of the grids from administrators? To address this challenge, this book discusses the dynamic provisioning technologies for community services deployed on the grid infrastructure. Specifically, we try to handle the availability of provisioning in terms of infrastructure and architecture, identify the dependency problems in distributed services, enhance the efficiency of provisioning in heterogeneous resources and interoperability among production grid middlewares. In more detail, we conclude the contributions as follows:

• First, from the view of infrastructure, we discuss Highly Available Dynamic Deployment infrastructure to handle the conflict between a nonstop serving capability and the necessity of provisioning for the grid systems. We make six criteria rules to address the key problems of the conflict. By proposing two deployment models (service and container-level deployment), HAND can efficiently serve the users' requests and provisioning requests at the same time.

• Second, using the infrastructure HAND, we introduce a new three-tier provisioning architecture, named Guardian. It can intelligently detect the different dependencies in the dynamic runtime environment of the grid systems. These dependencies include invocation, environment and deployment dependencies. In addition, Guardian provides a set of call back API for professional users who prefer higher availability. By practicing the maintenance of the CGSP system services (i.e., server provisioning), we can conclude that Guardian efficiently improves the global availability. Further, it can effectively manage different dependencies.

• Third, regarding the weakest-link effect existing in provisioning for heterogenous resources, we propose an asynchronous provisioning strategy for the Guardian system. The solution includes a set of specifications, the virtual maintainers and provisioning agents working in the three-tier architecture. It makes the provisioning processes transparent, intelligent and fault tolerant. Evaluating true image-processing services (i.e., user provisioning), Guardian can effectively tolerate heterogeneous resources and transient faults. Thereby, it enhances the global availability.

• Finally, we expand the provisioning technology to heterogeneous grid middleware. By using this, users can seamlessly deploy the user-level applications in different grids. It can dramatically decline the effects of resourceless problems. An image processing application running on three heterogeneous grid platforms is adopted to demonstrate the efficiency and capability of the proposed model. The result proves that the optimal solution can efficiently orchestrate current approaches.

All the models and ideas proposed in this book have been practically implemented in ChinaGrid applications. In particular, the HAND-C model has been adopted by Globus Alliance and released as a module in the latest Globus Toolkits. Furthermore, the GPE4CGSP and Guardian also contributed to open source projects for different usage. We hope that the contributions to dynamic provisioning can help administrators and developers of distributed computing.

8.2   Future Challenges

Many of the problems with dynamic provisioning of distributed systems will remain for a long time, perhaps for the next 20 years. We list several potential challenges in dynamic provisioning technologies as follows:

• *Intelligent Provisioning*: As the computing infrastructure grows on a world-wide level, provisioning technologies will hardly be able to handle the maintenance instructions in a reasonable time. Some new and intelligent technologies should be considered in the provisioning procedure. For example, an artificial neural network can effectively detect complicated problems and faults, collect necessary information and work out optimized solutions. By using artificial neurons, the provisioning technology might be directed to predictive maintenance and achieve its intrinsic goal mentioned by Mobley (1990).

• *Differentiated Provisioning for Virtual Machine and Physical Resources*: Due to the flexibility and facility of the virtual machines, many studies (Keahey *et al.*, 2005; Mendel Rosenblum, 2005) investigated applying on-demand VM provisioning for distributed applications. However, the I/O cost for transferring images of an operating system in a wide networking environment is still a challenge. In addition, how to combine the provisioning with physical resources to provide a powerful QoS, QoM-enabled computing environment? How to integrate with a modern job scheduler? These challenges demand much further effort.

• *Self-Organization, Self-Evolution and Self-Recovery Provisioning*: Recently, cloud computing (Marinos and Briscoe, 2009) became the main trend in the distributed computing community which focuses on flexibility and adaptability to customization. In 2007, IBM upgraded the HiPODS (Li *et al.*, 2006; Zhu *et al.*, 2009) project for cloud computing. Similarly, EC2 from Amazon (Garfinkel, 2007) and Google (Dean and Ghemawat, 2008) also contributed their efforts to cloud computing. According to the demands of self-organization, self-evolution and self-recovery (Kalyvianaki *et al.*, 2009), we need much more stable, reliable and intelligent dynamic provisioning technologies for cloud computing.

References

Dean J, Ghemawat S (2008) Mapreduce: Simplified data processing on large clusters. Communications of the ACM, 51: 107-113.

Garfinkel S (2007) An evaluation of Amazon's grid computing services: Ec2, s3 and sqs. Technical Report TR-08-07 S3.

Kalyvianaki E, Charalambous T, Hand S (2009) Self-adaptive and self-configured cpu resource provisioning for virtualized servers using Kalman filters. In: ICAC '09: Proceedings of the 6th International Conference on Autonomic computing. ACM, New York, NY, USA, pp. 117-126.

Keahey K, Foster I, Freeman T, Zhang XH, Galron D (2005) Virtual workspaces in the grid. Euro-Par 2005 Parallel Processing, 3648: 421-431.

Li Y, Qiu J, Sun K, Chen Y (2006) Modeling and verifying configuration in service deployment. In: Proceedings of IEEE International Conference on Services Computing 2006. IEEE Computer Society, Chicago, IL, USA, pp. 238-248.

Marinos A, Briscoe G (2009) Community cloud computing. In: CloudCom '09: Proceedings of the 1st International Conference on Cloud Computing, Springer-Verlag, Berlin, Heidelberg, pp. 472-484.

Mendel Rosenblum TG (2005) Virtual machine monitor: Current technology and future trends. IEEE Computer, 38(5): 39-47.

Mobley R (1990) An introduction to predictive maintenance. New York: Van Nostrand Reinhold, pp. 1-22.

Zhu J, Fang X, Guo Z, Niu MH, Cao F, Yue S, Liu QY (2009) Ibm cloud computing powering a smarter planet. In: CloudCom '09: Proceedings of the 1st International Conference on Cloud Computing, Springer-Verlag, Berlin, Heidelberg, pp. 621-625.

Glossary

Activate: Activate, one of the provisioning operations, means enabling one or a set of instances of a service in the distributed resources.

Active Object (AO): An AO, proposed by ProActive middleware, is actually a Java object that supports delivering parallel requests to remote resources seamlessly.

AND-dependency: AND-dependency describes the aggregating relation of other service components.

Apache Axis: Apache Axis is an open source XML processing engine framework. In practice it is an SOAP server to handle the Web service requests from heterogeneous clients. Currently it has been in C++ and Java.

Application Programming Interface (API): An API defines the boundary between the service and users in terms of the functions that users can call to make use of the service. It is an abstraction of the service such that the user is not required to understand the internal implementation and details.

Atomic Guardian: Atomic Guardian is an actual maintainer of the Guardian system. It mainly charges the notification, validation, session control and message processing.

Atomic Maintenance: Atomic Maintenance is an atomic operational procedure which will be running physically on a specific target. The sequential ID is unique for the target resource. The atomic maintenance is decoupled from the maintaining task.

Availability: Availability is a property of maintenance referring to the proportion of when time a system is in a functioning condition in the watching period. More specifically, the availability during the maintenance is the ratio of a system's available time to the longest maintaining time.

Business Process Execution Language (BPEL): BPEL (WS-BPEL), sponsored by OASIS, is an XML-based language to specify interactions with Web services. It provides convenience for users in composing the service components in an abstract process.

ChinaGrid: ChinaGrid, funded by the Ministry of Education in China, is an open scientific discovery infrastructure combining leadership class resources of 22 top universities in China to create an integrated, persistent computational resource.

Connected by high-performance CERNET, ChinaGrid integrates high-performance computers, data resources and tools, and high-end experimental facilities.

ChinaGrid SuperVision (CGSV): CGSV is the program launched to handle monitoring-related issues for the ChinaGrid project. Keeping in accordance with the latest efforts in SOA and grid communities, CGSV seeks a set of resource measurement and control services for the operation of ChinaGrid ecology.

ChinaGrid Support Platform (CGSP): CGSP is the common middleware for ChinaGrid. It includes several service components such as information services, data management services, execution management services and heterogeneous database services. It follows the design of Open Grid Service Architecture. Currently, it has been widely deployed in 12 universities and 5 main application grids in China.

ClassLoader: ClassLoader is an object that is responsible for loading classes inside JVM. It is essential for hot swap running objects and to identify the dependencies among services in a service container.

Cobweb Guardian: Cobweb Guardian, the coordinator of the Guardian system, works with multiple atomic Guardian to complete composite tasks.

Computing Element (CE): CE, defined in gLite middleware, is a set of computing resources localized at a site (i.e., a cluster, a computing farm).

Config: Config, one of the provisioning operations, means updating the configuration files of specific services to target resources and making them valid in the meantime.

Configuration Description, Deployment and Lifecycle Management (CDDLM): CDDLM is an international standard funded by Open Grid Forum (OGF). It is designed for the management, deployment and configuration of grid service lifecycles or inter-organization resources. In addition, it provides a framework that includes a language and methods that have the ability to describe system configuration and move systems, services and software towards desired configuration endpoints.

Configuration Management: Configuration Management is responsible for the frequent changes in dynamicity. For example, the newly joined resource node should be added to the serving list for the purpose of prompt invocation.

Consistency of Maintenance: Due to the complexity of the grid system, the maintenance of particular services is always propagated to many replications. Consistency is a measure to promise that the maintenance can be finished in a valid period or in the correct order.

Correctness of Normal Request: Correctness of Normal Request is a specification defined in asynchronous provisioning. It states that all the normal requests before, during, or after the maintaining (provisioning) tasks should be correctly handled by the service containers.

Critical Deployment Path: Critical Deployment Path is a minimal set of direct dependency sets in which the edges can link all of the vertices that a specific service depends on.

Deactivate: Deactivate, one of the provisioning operations, denotes disabling one or a set of running instances of a specific service.

Depended Degree: The Depended Degree of a specific service measures how much other services depend on it.

Depending Degree: The Depending Degree of a specific service records how much a service depends on other services.

Deploy: Deploy, one of the provisioning operations, refers to installing a service in a target system.

Deploy Approach Manager (DAM): DAM is a component of HAND. It takes as inputting a GAR file in Java archive format and provides local and remote mechanisms to assist users in deploying the GAR files.

Deployment Dependency: Deployment Dependency is a kind of service dependency. It includes the dependencies of software versions, the static requirement of configuration, and the compiling and bootstrapping dependencies of calling libraries.

Distributed Management Task Force (DMTF): DMTF is an international group to collaborate on the development, validation and promotion of systems management standards. DMTF management standards are critical to enabling management interoperability among multi-vendor systems, tools and solutions within the enterprise.

Dynamic Deployer Core (DDC): DDC is the kernel in realizing the dynamic deployment in HAND and meeting the six provisioning criteria. It is in charge of the deactivation (activation) of the services and container and the update of the runtime context in JVM.

Dynamic Deployment: Dynamic Deployment denotes the ability for remote clients to request the upload and deployment of new services into, or the undeployment of existing services from, existing grid containers. It is a special case of dynamic maintenance.

Dynamic Maintenance: Dynamic Maintenance includes the operations (e.g. deploying, undeploying, and so forth) to large-scale service components in the runtime. The dynamicity of maintenance means that the maintenance will not affect the execution of existing components and promises as little as possible downtime. Normally, the maintaining requests are delivered by the administrators and provisioning modules.

Dynamic Reconfiguration: Dynamic Reconfiguration means the distributed system can continuously evolve without recompiling and can restart after reconstruction.

Dynamicity: Dynamicity is a property of maintenance meaning the provisioning task should guarantee correctness when grid resources leave or join in occasionally.

Enabling Grids for E-science (EGEE): EGEE is one of the biggest grid projects funded by the European Commission. It hired the LCG-2 based on GT2 and gLite as the middleware to manage the grid resources.

Environment Dependency: Environment Dependency is a kind of service dependency that happens when deploying services to heterogeneous hosting environments. It considers the possible effects when two or more service instances are running in the same environment.

Fault Tolerance: Fault Tolerance is a property of maintenance meaning the provisioning procedure should tolerate uncertain factors including unstable network latency and emergency events.

General Running Service (GRS): GRS is a Web service deployed in CGSP middleware. Its main function is wrapping the legacy programs in heterogenous platforms as a standard Web service or WSRF-compliant Web services. Sequentially, the legacy applications can be easily migrated to grids.

gLite: gLite, sponsored by EGEE, is a grid middleware that provides a framework for building grid applications that tap into the power of distributed computing and storage resources across the Internet.

Globus Toolkit (GT): GT is an open source software toolkit for developing grid-based applications. More information is available at http://www.globus.org/.

GPE4CGSP: GPE4CGSP is an interactive module that coordinates the job requests between ChinaGrid underlying resources and the ones distributed in alien grids.

Grid: Grid is a large-scale geographically distributed hardware and software infrastructure composed of heterogeneous networked resources owned and shared by multiple administrative organizations which are coordinated to provide transparent, dependable, pervasive and consistent computing support to a wide range of applications.

Grid Archive (GAR): GAR is the service package file for deployment and provisioning. Normally, a GAR file includes the related resources, descriptors (WSDD and configurations) and binary installations.

GridBean: GridBean, issued in GPE, is a common submitting interface for end users. By contacting with GridBean, users can invoke and access remote applications in the Application Client or Expert Client freely.

GridFTP: Developed by Globus Toolkit team, GridFTP is a distributed file transferring protocol to provide high security and efficiency.

Grid Parallel Programming Interface (GridPPI): GridPPI is a set of AIP provided by CGSP to enable end users, especially developers, to implement grid-enabled parallel applications.

Grid Programming Environment (GPE): GPE is proposed by Intel Corporation to realize a common user interface for client developers and users. By using GPE library, a user can use a common GridBean to submit a grid job to different grid platforms.

Grid Resources: Grid resources are the IT infrastructure which can be leased for expert domains computation. Examples include various computational machines, instruments, storage equipment, and so on.

Grid Resource Allocation Manager (GRAM): GRAM is the kernel module of Globus Toolkit's execution management. Actually, it is a remote execution coordinator which periodically reports status for the resource execution. By providing open API for a lower layer execution system, GRAM supports several legacy distributed resource managers such as PBS, LSF and Loadleveler.

Grid Resource Lifecycle: A grid resource inside a dynamic provisioning system includes four different states. They are (i) the resources which have not deployed any software and even operating systems; (ii) the resources which have not deployed related services but have deployed specific grid platforms; (iii) resources which have deployed related services and are available for accepting the user's requests; (iv) the resources which have been leased by some other application.

Grid Security Infrastructure (GSI): GSI, sponsored by Globus Alliance, is a specification for secret, tamper-proof, delegatable communication between software in a grid computing environment. By using digital signature technology, it provides the basic authentication function for grid infrastructure. Also, GSI provides transport layer and/or message-level security for different secure demands.

GT4: GT4 is the version 4.0 of Globus Toolkit. It is based on the Web Services Resource Framework Specification. Recently, the latest version of GT 5.0 has been released.

HAND-C: The HAND infrastructure runs under container-level.

HAND-S: The HAND infrastructure runs under service-level.

Heterogeneity: The provisioning operation should transparently deal with different operating systems, different architectures and different compiler versions.

Heterogeneous Database (HDB): HDB is a module in CGSP to support interoperations among different and distributed databases in other grid domains. Similar to OGSA-DAI defined in OGSA, it provides a set of API to help ChinaGrid developers transparently access heterogeneous database management systems.

Heterogeneous Grid Platforms: Heterogeneous Grid Platforms means the computational infrastructures that are equipped with different middleware software. Normally, the grid middlewares follow the OGSA standards and include the functionalities of deployment, registration, discovery, running and monitoring the grid infrastructure and applications.

Highly Available Dynamic Deployment (HAND): HAND is a kernel module in CGSP and GT's service container. As the infrastructure of dynamic provisioning, HAND provides service and container-level hot replacement of service components deployed on containers.

Hot Deploy-Enabled Infrastructure: It means the computing infrastructure supports dynamically swap software components without shutting down the whole system.

Implicational Maintaining Relationship: Implicational Maintaining Relationship describes the possible hidden maintenances that should be done first for a specific resource. It should be detected automatically for integrity of maintenance.

Improved Ratio: Improved Ratio depicts the improved utilization of a specific maintaining approach against the total maintaining time for all related resources in synchronous mode.

Interoperability: Interoperability is a property referring to the ability of diverse grids and organizations to work together (inter-operate).

Invocation Dependency: Invocation Dependency is a kind of service dependency that happens among composite Web services during the runtime.

Normally, it includes several composite relations, such as AND-dependency, XOR-dependency and OR-dependency. By composing these dependent relations, we can construct enough complicated logic flows among services.

Job Submission Description Language (JSDL): JSDL is a specification proposed by OGF to describe the job submitting interfaces at a standard level. Currently, this specification has been widely implemented by UNICORE, CGSP and the other main grid platforms.

LHC Computing Grid (LCG): LCG, designed by CERN, is a distribution grid to handle the massive amounts of data produced by the Large Hadron Collider (LHC). The EGEE project provides the distributed computing resources for LCG.

Maintaining Duration: Maintaining Duration denotes the duration from the start of maintenance to the time when the first related resource is available.

Maintaining Task: Maintaining Task is an operational request from a user or an administrator, which consists of (i) the global and unique maintaining sequence id; (ii) the collection of services it plans to maintain, (iii) the planned computational nodes related to target service components and (iv) the collection of maintaining operations such as deploying, backup, re-configuring, and so forth.

Maintaining Stack: Maintaining Stack is designed to support asynchronous maintenance. It stores all of the atomic maintenances that are decoupled from the virtual maintainer.

Monitoring and Discovery Service (MDS): MDS is a kernel module of Globus Toolkit's information services. It supports the publishing and querying of grid resources information. It is designed in a three-layer architecture which consists of Information Provider (IP), Grid Resource Information Service (GRIS) and Grid Information Index Service (GIIS) respectively.

N1 Service Provisioning System (SPS): N1 SPS, sponsored by SUN, automates the deployment of multi-tier applications across heterogeneous resources. The highlight of N1 SPS is that it can simulate the deployment process on target systems prior to actually implementing the changes, to ensure successful delivery. In addition, the version control and role-based access control can help users construct applications efficiently.

Node Level: The maintenance at node level is from the global viewpoint. The reloading or pending operations at this level will issue a group of computing nodes. It balances the maintaining policies among the different containers.

OGSA-DAI: OGSA-DAI is motivated to share data resources to enable collaboration. Namely, it belongs to OGSA architecture. It mainly charges the data access, transformation, integration and delivery.

Open Grid Forum (OGF): OGF was an international open organization combined from Global Grid Forum (GGF) and Enterprise Grid Alliance in 2006. Its responsibilities include (i) organizing end users, developers and providers of the grid community, (ii) maintaining and writing related open standards. The standards of OGSA, OGSI and JSDL are initialized by OGF.

Open Grid Service Architecture (OGSA): OGSA is a refinement of the Web services architecture for grid computing. From a high level architectural viewpoint, it describes a service-oriented approach, namely grid services, to address the integration of distributed, heterogeneous and dynamic resources.

OR-dependency: OR-dependency is a kind of composing logic for service components in a distributed environment. It means the request will successfully be delivered to one of the succeeding resources if the condition can be matched by any of the succeeding candidates.

Organization for the Advancement of Structured Information Standards (OASIS): OASIS is a not-for-profit consortium that drives the development, convergence and adoption of open standards for the global information society.

ProActive: ProActive, developed by INRIA, is a grid middleware implemented in Java. It is designed for parallel, distributed and multi-threaded computing. Unlike other gird middleware, it concentrates more on programming models instead of the constructing mechanisms. It promotes the ideas of active objects and groups to help developers easily build parallel applications.

Publish: Publish, one of the provisioning operations, is for registering service information to a public information center such as UDDI or CGSP information service.

Quality of Manageability: Quality of Manageability is a measure of the ability to manage a system component. QoM measures include the number of lines of configuration code (LOC) for deployment, the number of steps involved in deployment, LOC to express configuration changes and the time to develop, deploy and make a change.

Query Task: Query Task in dynamic provisioning is a querying procedure from the computational resource to its provisioning worker.

Remote Method Invocation (RMI): RMI refers to a Java API for calling the methods of remote Java objects on different hosts. More information is available at http://java.sun.com/products/jdk/rmi/.

Replica Location Service (RLS): RLS is the replication management component inside Globus Toolkits. By registering with RLS, a file and its replicas can be automatically created and deleted according to proper strategies.

Resourceless Phenomenon: Resourceless Phenomenon defined in this book means that the grid infrastructure can't provide adequate available resources to process the jobs when no further maintenances or interoperations are issued.

Result Group: Result Group in ProActive is transparently built at invocation time of a normal group, with a future for each elementary reply.

Runtime Migration: Runtime Migration means cloning a proper instance of some service components to a new computational node. This functionality is usually required for fault tolerance and a highly reliable system.

Saved Server Time: Saved Server Time represents the sum of the saved time for each related resource. Specifically, it denotes the duration between the available time of the specific resource and the completed time for all related maintenances.

Scalability: Scalability is a property of maintenance referring to the provisioning tasks that can be correctly propagated to thousands, even millions of nodes.

Security: Security is a property of maintenance referring to the provisioning operation that should be strictly authorized to trusted members of a specific VO.

Server Provisioning: Server Provisioning means the preparation of a distributed application's infrastructure which normally constructs group of servers.

Service Component: Service Component in service provisioning/mainatenance is defined as a quadruple form that includes (i) a set of provided service functions, (ii) the implementations of service, (iii) the static data (i.e., configurations, endpoint location and deployment descriptor), (iv) the dynamic data (i.e., the runtime parameters, the staging data and the QoS demands).

Service-/Container-/Global-Level of Maintenance: The maintenance of any new service components involves reloading (reinitializing and reconfiguring) the service (or container or whole grid respectively).

Service Dependency: The correct execution of a service component is always dependent on the hosting environment, the dependent calling services and the dependent deployment service respectively.

Service Dependency Matrix (SDM): SDM is an $n \times n$ mesh. Each element in the matrix is defined as boolean and denotes 1 (*true*) when the two related services are dependent.

Service Oriented Architecture (SOA): SOA is a group of design principles and models for distributed computing. The advantages of SOA include (i) loosely coupled service components, (ii) high reusability of components and (iii) seamless invocations among heterogeneous platforms.

Service Package Manager (SPM): SPM is the component in HAND to manage the lifecycle of grid service packages. Normally, it is unique in a specific VO.

Service Provisioning: Service Provisioning is in charge of deploying the new service components, upgrading the existing service components and uninstalling the deployed service components from the computational system dynamically upon the user's demand and QoS requirements.

Service Provisioning Markup Language (SPML): SPML, released by OASIS, is a standard providing an XML framework for managing the provisioning and allocation of identity information and system resources within and between organizations.

Simple Object Access Protocol (SOAP): SOAP, sponsored by W3C, is a protocol specification for exchanging structured information in the implementation of Web services on the Internet. Similar to WSDL and UDDI, it is a principle standard of Web services defined in XML format. SOAP messages can be transferred in several open networking protocols including SMTP and HTTP.

Six Criteria of HAND: At the infrastructure level, the six criteria are proposed to guarantee the correct procession of normal service requests and provisioning/maintenance requests. This can effectively maintain the integrity, availability and deadlock-free of the grid infrastructure during maintenance.

Storage Element (SE): SE provides uniform access to data storage resources registered in gLite middleware.

Sync Maintenance: The maintenance or provisioning processes run in a synchronous mode. For instance, the predecessor provisioning process will not be activated until all of the proceeding provisioning processes are completed successfully.

Tivoli Provisioning Manager (TPM): TPM, implemented by IBM, is a common usage provisioning system that enhances usability for executing changes while keeping server and desktop software compliant. It helps organizations with provisioning, configuration and maintenance of servers, virtual servers and other resources. It supports operating system provisioning, software provisioning and storage provisioning.

Transient Fault: Transient Fault denotes a temporal or short failure happening to the target servers during the maintaining procedure.

Undeploy: Undeploy, one of the provisioning operations, denotes uninstalling a service from the target system.

UNICORE: UNICORE is a vertically integrated grid middleware for the German D-Grid. It provides a seamless, secure and intuitive access to resources in a distributed environment for end users. In addition, it constructs an easy relocation of computer jobs to different platforms, for both end users and grid sites.

Uniform Agreement: Uniform Agreement is a specification introduced in asynchronous provisioning. It means that once a provisioning worker executes a correct provisioning/maintaining task, all live provisioning works will eventually roll the status forward to the latest task.

Uniform Integrity: Uniform Integrity is a specification introduced in asynchronous provisioning. It denotes that, for any target resources, the assigned provisioning task will be executed exclusively once.

Uniform Maintaining Order: Uniform Maintaining Order is a specification defined in asynchronous provisioning. It means that each maintaining task owns a unique execution order. All the tasks should sequentially be executed according to the assigned order on different resources.

Universal Description, Discovery and Integration (UDDI): UDDI, sponsored by OASIS, is a platform-independent XML-based registry standard for Web services. It enables Web service instances to publish service listings, discover others and define the accessing approaches in a standard format. As one of three fundamental standards of Web services, the UDDI registers the WSDL from publishers and permits requesters access to these services by SOAP protocol.

Upgrade: Upgrade, one of the provisioning operations, means installing a newer version or a patch of a service in a specific system where we have installed the service.

Usability: Usability is a property of maintenance referring to the provisioning interface that should be simple and the propagation of instructions that should be transparent to end users.

User-Level Middleware: User-Level Middleware is the access point to the gLite grid in the user interface.

User Provisioning: User Provisioning is a preparation procedure to help end users more quickly, more cheaply and more securely construct an application running environment.

U-Site: U-Site in UNICORE is an abstract layer which provides a set of service interfaces and coordinates the requests from the user-tier to V-Sites.

VEGA: VEGA grid is a grid middleware developed by the Institute of Computing Technology, Chinese Academy of Sciences. By introducing grid-enabling servers, grid routers, grid switches, grid address spaces, grid process (grip), grid community (agora), and GSML software, the VEGA architecture can view a grid as a computer system at the hardware and operating system level.

Virtual Maintainer: Virtual Maintainer is an essential component of an asynchronous provisioning model. Its responsibilities include decoupling the maintaining task into atomic maintenances and assigning the maintenance order to each task. In addition, it also charges the recovery works once a maintaining task is filed.

Virtual Nodes: Virtual Nodes defined in ProActive are the actual executing units that are normally identified as a simple string name.

Virtual Organization (VO): VO is a dynamic set of personal users and/or organizations with a set of resource-sharing rules and conditions. By attending the specific VO, the users geographically distributed in different realistic organizations can access the shared resources seamlessly.

Virtual Workspace Service (VWS): VWS, sponsored by Globus Alliance, is a management service for provisioning virtual machines among clusters and grids.

V-Site: V-Site is one of the essential components of UNICORE that wraps the heterogeneous computing resources as the common target system.

Weakest-Link Effect: Weakest-Link Effect refers to the phenomenon whereby the slowest provisioning processes in the maintaining list will eventually delay the whole procedure of maintenance and provisioning.

Web Service Deployment Descriptor (WSDD): WSDD is an XML language to describe the services deployed on the service processing engine (e.g. Apache AXIS). Users can add customized definitions inside the WSDD file to meet optional handlers on engines.

Web Service Resource Framework (WSRF): WSRF, released by OASIS, is a set of Web service standards to support the stateful features of normal Web services. It consists of six components that are WS-Resource, WS-ResourceProperties, WS-ResourceLifetime, WS-BaseFaults, WS-ServiceGroup, WS-Notification. With the implementation of WSRF, Web services can support more complicated grid applications. Currently, many popular grid middlewares have implemented WSRF. The representations include Globus Toolkit, CGSP, IBM WebSphere Application Server, and so forth.

Web Services Description Language (WSDL): WSDL, sponsored by W3C, is one of the fundamental standards of Web services. It is XML-based and it defines the Web services as collections of endpoints or ports. Due to the scandalization of accessing interfaces, it greatly enhances the reusability of the service component. Normally, it works with the other two fundamental standards of Web services, i.e., SOAP and UDDI.

Web Services Distributed Management (WSDM): WSDM, released by OASIS, is a Web service standard to manage the distributed Web services. It includes two sub-specifications, Management Using Web Services (MUWS) and Management of Web Services (MOWS). MUWS defines how to represent and access the manageability interfaces of resources as Web services. By using MUWS, MOWS defines the approach for managing Web services as resources and how to describe and access the manageability.

Workload Management System (WMS): In gLite middleware, WMS distributed in the client layer is for accepting user jobs, to assign them to the most appropriate computing element, to record their status and retrieve their output.

World Wide Web Consortium (W3C): W3C is an international community where member organizations, a full-time staff and the public work together to develop Web standards.

XOR-dependency: XOR-dependency means the replication relationship. For instance, the requests to a composite service will be delivered randomly to the depending components.

Index

Printed in the United States
By Bookmasters

Printed in the United States
By Bookmasters